STUDYING FILMS

ALSO AVAILABLE IN THIS SERIES

FORTHCOMING

STUDYING PAN'S LABYRINTH

Tanya Jones

Dedication

To Molly and Richard, my mum and dad. In thanks for many years of encouragement and support.

First published in 2010; this edition first published 2017 by
Auteur, 24 Hartwell Crescent, Leighton Buzzard LU7 1NP
www.auteur.co.uk
Copyright © Auteur 2010; 2017

Series design: Nikki Hamlett
All DVD framegrabs taken from the Region 2 DVD edition of *Pan's Labyrinth* available from Optimum Home Entertainment.
Set by Cassels Design
Printed and bound in the UK

British Library Cataloguing-in-Publication Data
A catalogue record for this book is available from the British Library

ISBN 978-1-906733-30-8

Contents

Studying *Pan's Labyrinth* Factsheet

Pan's Labyrinth (*El labertino del fauno*) 2006 (Mexico)
Running Time   118 mins
Certificate   15 (UK); R (US)
Production Company   Tequila Gang, Esperanto Films
Distributor   Optimum Releasing UK, Picturehouse US

Key Credits

Writer/ Director/ Producer	Guillermo del Toro
Producers	Bertha Navarro, Alfonso Cuaron, Frida Torresblanco, Alvaro Augustin
Director of Photography	Guillermo Navarro
Production Designer	Eugenio Caballero
Original Music	Javier Navarrete
Editing	Bernat Vilaplana
Special Effects Supervisor	David Marti

Cast

Ofelia	Ivana Baquero
Vidal	Sergi Lopez
Mercedes	Maribel Verdu
Carmen	Ariadna Gil
Faun/ Pale Man	Doug Jones

Synopsis

It is 1944; Ofelia is uprooted and sent with her mother to a Fascist military outpost run by her step-father. Ofelia's mother is pregnant with Ofelia's brother. In order to cope with the loneliness, isolation and fear that characterise Ofelia's new home, she absorbs herself in a rich fantasy world. In this world she is given three tasks. Being successful at these tasks will mean that Ofelia can be restored to her rightful place as a Princess in another world. Despite support from her step-father Captain Vidal's servant, Mercedes, and the rising strength of the resistance movement, Ofelia's end is tragic.

Budget

13,500,000 Euros

Release Strategy

Pan's Labyrinth was first shown at the 2006 Cannes Film Festival on 27 May 2006. It premiered in the UK at the London FrightFest Film Festival on 25 August 2006. Its first general release was in Spain on 11 October 2006.

INTRODUCTION

Del Toro and the Faun

What is it about *Pan's Labyrinth* that makes it deserving of a close study? Is it the stunning visual beauty of the film? Is it the haunting lullaby theme that never fails to evoke the tragedy of Ofelia's position? Is it the masterful combining of fantasy and horror conventions to produce a barbed, threatening, but beautiful, cinematic landscape? *Pan's Labyrinth* is a very challenging piece of film-making. It has an ideological, as well as emotional impetus. It presents the ravaging impact of Spanish Fascism distilled into a corner of rural Spain, as well as the harrowing journey of our doomed protagonist, Ofelia. Studying *Pan's Labyrinth* presents all of the above as reasons for a close analysis of this film. Any one of these reasons would be justification enough; the combination of all of them makes it an essential text. This guide aims to offer two things: firstly, a clear and comprehensive framework for the study of any single film; and secondly, an investigation into the wonderful complexities of this text.

Guillermo del Toro was born in Guadalajara, Mexico, in 1964. He was a founding member of the Film Studies Centre and, in his hometown, the Muesta del Cine Mexicano (Mexican film Festival). Del Toro studied scriptwriting and special effects, eventually setting up his own special effects company, called Necropia. It was through Necropia, that del Toro met the producer Bertha Navarro. Alongside Navarro, with Laura Esquival and Rosa Bosch, del Toro then set up the production company, The Tequilla Gang.

Cronos (1993) was del Toro's first film as director. (Alongside Alfonso Arau's 1992 film *Like Water for Chocolate, Cronos* is often credited with putting Mexican Cinema back onto the world stage.) Ostensibly a vampire film about the terrible cost of immortality, this film also exhibits del Toro's more political signature. Not only does it deal with the great metaphysical questions of an individual's relationship with life and death, but it can also be read as a comment on the vampiric relationship between one culture or community and another, the latter being a theme that is also explored in del Toro's later Spanish language films. Another similarity between *Cronos* and del Toro's later work is the construction of a fantasy suffused reality:

> **'I did not set *Cronos* in any real world; I don't try and represent reality exactly as it is. I always try to take it a couple of notches above.'** (del Toro in Wood, 2006)

Cronos went on to win a Critic's Week Award at the 1993 Cannes Film Festival. *The Devil's Backbone* (2001) is set in an orphanage and has the Spanish Civil War as its back-drop. The theme of the vulnerable child evident within *Cronos*, is again exploited in *The Devil's Backbone*; and later, of course, in *Pan's Labyrinth*. The orphanage in *The Devil's Backbone* is isolated and lonely. The children are abandoned to the environment, the political context and the ghosts. Del Toro's Spanish language films pitch children up against dark forces and are often brutal in their depiction of what happens when these forces of darkness are not treated with caution. Del Toro acknowledges that his films deliberately place children in hazardous scenarios:

> **'Horror is an extension of the fairytale, and in fairytales ogres and wolves eat children and I think that it goes to the roots of storytelling, to have children as vulnerable.'** (ibid.)

Cronos and *The Devil's Backbone* may be eight years apart, but they share key features of the del Toro signature. Both utilise horror conventions. The former utilises the vampire myth and the latter presents a ghost story, but both of these films present the quest for truth and the solutions to enigmas established in the film's back-stories. Carlos the child protagonist in *The Devil's Backbone* and the granddaughter Aurora in *Cronos*, both act as powerful filters through which the audience can understand the inhumane and destructive nature of the adult world. As in *Pan's Labyrinth*, the child in these films is placed in front of the monstrous so that the viewer is even more aware of the innocence that can be lost. *Cronos* and *The Devil's Backbone* also share a socio-political impetus with *Pan's Labyrinth*. It is not merely individuals that create horror, but societies, too. Del Toro's implication of cultural vampirism in *Cronos* is extended in *The Devil's Backbone* to include a comment about how a political conflict, such as the Spanish Civil War, can suck the life blood out of a country. In *Pan's Labyrinth*, of course, the literal and figurative death of Ofelia is a consequence of the political situation of Spain at that time.

Del Toro's English speaking films, which include *Mimic* (1997), *Blade II* (2002), *Hellboy* (2004), *Pacific Rim* (2013) and *Crimson Peak* (2015) have some similarities to the Spanish work. *Hellboy*, in particular, included a personal vision, which was not lost within the major financing of the film. Fantasy, horror and gothic horror combine to form the backdrop to this story about a lonely, abused and ostracised child (the 'Hellboy'). As del Toro's first step into the world of Hollywood film-making, *Mimic* was a less-than-wholly rewarding experience. Creative differences with producers Dimension Films meant that del Toro did not feel that he had creative control and this experience was a key contributory factor for his return to Spanish language film-making.

Guillermo del Toro is a director who brings his own particular skills and experiences to the cinematic canvas. Trained in special effects, his films employ extraordinary visuals to create fantasy worlds. Del Toro's own childhood experience of fairy stories, gothic tales, real stories about the Spanish Civil War and horror cinema, all contribute to his vision. If horror and fantasy are indeed the perfect conduits for political statement, then del Toro is an arch exponent. *Pan's Labyrinth* takes up the baton from *Cronos* and *The Devil's Backbone* on all of the above counts.

NARRATIVE

The start of Ofelia's journey

The study of narrative is the exploration of how a story is structured and organised. This structuring and organisation functions to create meaning and generate a particular response from the audience. There are various means by which a film's narrative can be analysed. These break a film down into specific sections that contain particular events and have particular functions. The narrative theory formulated by Tzvetan Todorov (1969) in his literary and cultural criticism, defined three basic stages of a narrative's structure. In very basic terms, a state of Equilibrium exists at the beginning of a story. This then is disrupted, becoming a Disequilibrium. The narrative eventually resolves and a New Equilibrium is created. Of course, this three stage structure, once translated into an actual narrative, becomes more complex and individualised.

The term 'equilibrium' implies calm. The status quo is intact and the characters are safe at this point in the narrative structure. *Pan's Labyrinth*, however, begins with the image of a dead child, so its narrative structure can be read as retrospective; a retelling of what brings Ofelia to this tragic position. This structural device is not referred to again, either implicitly or explicitly, but it does present a story being told and that story is Ofelia's. At the chronological beginning of *Pan's Labyrinth*, Ofelia's state of equilibrium is thus already compromised. Our first image of Ofelia is a tragic one. She is bleeding and wounded. The audience then sees the fantasy world, but this is not enough to remove the hideous image of a dying child. She is then seen on the road to her step-father's house. Her mother is pregnant by Vidal and Ofelia is seen from the outset reading fairy stories and resisting the new future her mother has planned for her. Ofelia is not safe at the beginning of the narrative. Her back-story, which we discover later, of a tailor father and a loving home, is actually the period of equilibrium for this character.

Ofelia's situation is thus already 'disrupted' by the time she gets to the Mill, meets Vidal and enters into the full disequilibrium. As characters within Todorov's second narrative stage, the Fascists (Vidal in particular) act as the agents of disruption. They are oppressive, repressive and have already destroyed the political equilibrium that existed in pre-Fascist Spain. The Faun, as stated elsewhere in this study guide, cannot be considered a moral barometer, precisely because of its moral ambiguity. Neither can it be seen as an agent of re-instatement of peace and calm. The Faun propels Ofelia towards her dual fate. The quests culminate in two events. In the 'real' narrative, Vidal shoots Ofelia. In the fantasy narrative, she takes her rightful place alongside her parents and brother.

The new equilibrium of *Pan's Labyrinth* within the 'real' narrative sees Mercedes and her brother confront Vidal. He is killed and Ofelia's brother is taken to live a new life with the resistance. In the fantasy narrative, the predictions within the opening fairy story are fulfilled and Ofelia enters her kingdom. What is strikingly unusual about del Toro's narrative is that the child dies. She is not just vulnerable and threatened, as is perhaps to be expected, but she is shot and killed. New equilibriums are often built on sacrifices made during the disequilibrium section of a narrative. What is shocking about the end of this film is that in the 'real' world, political turmoil is only halted by the sacrifice of Ofelia. A damning statement from del Toro, perhaps, about what is necessary in the face of a relentless political monster, such as Fascism.

An alternative breakdown of the structure of a narrative, offers five significant sections for analysis: Exposition, Development, Complication, Climax and Resolution (Todorov, ibid.). These headings, too, can be usefully applied to *Pan's Labyrinth*. The exposition part of a film's narrative introduces the setting and the characters to the film audience.

The opening images of the film introduce the viewer to the date, 1944, to the political situation in Spain, to a dying Ofelia and to the fantasy world. The introduction of Ofelia's primary relationship, ie. with her mother, also comes in this section.

In the development stage of a film the storyline is expanded and the audience is introduced to more characters. In the development section of *Pan's Labyrinth*, the audience is introduced to Vidal, the Fascists, Mercedes and the resistance movement. We are also introduced to the Faun and the quest narrative commences. Ofelia's relationship with Mercedes develops, but her mother's pregnancy becomes more life threatening. During the complication stage of the film's narrative, we are presented with (an) event(s) that will adversely affect the lives of the main protagonists within a film. With a dense and intricately plotted film like *Pan's Labyrinth* there are events that have a dramatic impact rather than one single event. However, the most significant event in this section of the narrative must be the death of Ofelia's mother. Her loss is unbearable for Ofelia who throws herself entirely into the constructed truths of the Labyrinth. The death of the mother in fairy stories, and indeed most other narratives, signals a period of extreme danger and emotional turbulence for the child left behind. Vidal also reacts strongly to his wife's death, but his reaction is to justify his own actions even more vehemently, now that he has an heir to take on his role and ideology.

Ofelia withholds her brother from the Faun

At the climax of a film's narrative, dramatic tension is at its height and the secrets or enigmas of the previous action are revealed. This is also the point in the film where there is often a confrontation between the two (usually) characters that represent 'good' and 'evil' in the story. In *Pan's Labyrinth*, this is the section of the narrative in which Ofelia discovers the true nature of the Faun's tasks. She finally understands that she must lose her own future, in order to save that of her brother. The climactic section of this film justifies her death in sacrificial and redemptive terms. Ofelia confronts both the Faun and Vidal. She refuses to give up her brother to the Faun, is told the truth and succeeds in her quest. Ofelia and the Faun's dialogue reveals the secrets of the narrative and is transformative. Ofelia's second confrontation is with the much less morally ambiguous Vidal. Coded as the monster from the outset of the film, by his brutality to the rabbit poachers and Dr Ferriero and his cave/inferno-like room, he takes Ofelia's life without remorse or emotion.

The end of a film usually holds its resolution: the sequence where stability is re-established and a form of calm has been restored. As has been discussed previously, the resolution section of *Pan's Labyrinth* actually includes two scenarios. Both narratives are resolved, it's just that one demands the tragic death of Ofelia to achieve its goal.

With a film so firmly rooted in a particular historical period, it is important to be aware of what happened at that time. Obviously, *Pan's Labyrinth* is not a documentary, or a war film as we generally imagine one. It is a film that juxtaposes fantasy and extremely harsh reality in order to then make comments about the nature of both. From 1936 to 1939, Spain experienced the Spanish Civil War. This was an incredibly complicated and turbulent period within Spanish history, which saw right-wing generals attempt to overthrow the newly democratically elected leftist government. These rebel Nationalists were headed by Francisco Franco and were supported by the Catholic Church and Spain's land-owning elite. With significant aid and armed support from both Mussolini in Italy and Hitler in Germany, the right was eventually successful and General Franco controlled Spain until his death in 1975. Del Toro's film uses 1944 Spain as its backdrop. It presents rural Spain as a place of conflict and repression, with Fascist troops attempting to 'put down' the resistance fighters. It was the stories of and from Spanish exiles, who came to Mexico after Franco's take over, and the impact that these individuals had on Mexican culture, that helped spark del Toro's interest in the period.

In terms of structure and content, *Pan's Labyrinth* owes much to traditional fairy tales. The kinds of tale del Toro are most influenced by are those that contain dark and gruesome elements. His cinematic canvas draws from the Brothers Grimm and the sinister visuals of their work and others like them. In Grimm fairy stories, trees have savage arms for branches and their roots contain monsters. The striking visuals of these dark fairy tale worlds and their focus on moral questions, are elements that are clearly evident in *Pan's Labyrinth*. Del Toro stated that:

> **'*Pan's Labyrinth* uses fantasy and the supernatural to confront the malevolence and violence of the real world (Spain under Franco).'**
> (Podcast, www.panslabyrinth.com)

Ofelia is obsessed with fairy stories and she constructs her own fairy world in order to deal with the brutality surrounding her. In the Fascist world of Ofelia's step-father Vidal, death and life exist in close proximity, and in the world of fairy tales the same dynamic occurs; either death or life can be the consequence of the quests and tasks set up within the narrative. Whether using a critical framework, such as Vladimir Propp's analysis of the basic structures of fairy tales (as first espoused in *Morphology of the Folk Tale*, 1928) or from personal experience of fairy stories, it is clear that *Pan's Labyrinth* utilises fairy tale narrative conventions. Propp's Russian Formalist approach to analysing the fairy tale meant that he broke narrative down into smaller and smaller constituent elements, in order eventually to distil the fairy story to its core components. Formalist approaches to the study of literary texts first came about as a response to Romanticist approaches, which focused on the creative individual behind the text and privileged the individual genius of the *auteur*. Formalism, in contrast, focused on the constituent elements of the text, e.g. its grammar, imagery and narrative components. Who created the text and in what socio/political context was not what the Formalists highlighted. In terms of character roles within a narrative, Propp identified seven key character types within a fairy story:

1. **The hero or victim/seeker hero.** This character takes up the quest, succeeds and generally marries the Princess at the end of the narrative.

2. **The false hero**. The character that tries to take credit for the hero's actions and attempts to marry the Princess.

3. **The villain**. Struggles against the hero and attempts to thwart his/her success.

4. **The donor**. Has similarities to the helper character, as the donor can give the magical challenge to the hero or give him/her a magical object to help them.

5. **The (magical) helper**. His character helps the hero in their quest.

6. **The dispatcher**. This character identifies a lack or gap in the hero's world at the beginning of the story and sends him/her off to complete the task.

7. **The Princess and her father**. These characters have a very close bond. It can be the father who gives the task to the hero and the prize is often the hand of the princess in marriage. The drive of the narrative might also be towards a reunion of the Princess and the father. The Princess might also be unknowing of her true heritage.

Creatures in classic tales can include goblins, elves, trolls, animals and talking animals. Ofelia encounters an enormous toad, fairies, a Mandrake baby, the monstrous Pale Man and, of course, the Faun itself. She occupies the Princess and the hero(ine) position in the narrative and holding with the classic convention, she is initially oblivious to her true identity. In the world of the labyrinth her real father is the King, her mother the Queen and her infant brother the Prince. The initially dispossessed family eventually takes back their true position, but not until the quest has been successful. Ofelia is the heroine of the piece. She is not capable of violence, but she is capable of disobedience; a character trait that is essential within the morally dubious worlds of the film. Characters like Ofelia and Mercedes, who do not succumb to Vidal's rule of law, as well as Doctor Ferreiro who explicitly rejects Vidal's codes, provide the transgression that is necessary to break the 'evil spell' within the world of *Pan's Labyrinth*.

Ofelia is given three tasks, the classic trilogy of the quest. There are other 'threes' in the film: three fairies, three doors behind which there is one key in the Pale Man's lair. There are 'threes' in the real world, too. The stuttering prisoner is told by Vidal to count to three in order to win his freedom. There are three main female characters. Ofelia's three tasks are ever more challenging and dangerous. They require her to believe in their reality and their worth. Ofelia is the endangered child whose strength of purpose and belief in the truth of her birthright eventually bring about resolution in the form of re-union with her true family. Of course, in del Toro's translation of these narrative conventions, the danger for Ofelia is not solely from the creatures, but from Vidal. As representative of the brutality of Fascism, he is the most dangerous of all and kills the Princess/ heroine in his own quest to take control of his son and by extension his particular region of Spain. In *Pan's Labyrinth*, Vidal and his troops are the relentless, violent force of Fascist ideology. The monsters in the fairy tale narrative are representations of the monstrous in the real world. Fairy stories make violence, evil and inhumanity palpable and visual through the creation of hideous creatures that on the outside are as repellent as they are on the inside. In the real world the evil within is more difficult to spot and the fantasy elements of *Pan's Labyrinth* help Ofelia to see what she is dealing with by making who and what is dangerous distinct.

The moral ambiguity that exists in classic fairy story narratives also exists within del Toro's film. Whether the Faun is the (magic) helper of Propp's character types or, in fact, the villain of the piece, is unclear at times. It is enigmatic, the holder of secrets, cruel at times and then comforting. Its role is to give agency to the quest and motivate Ofelia towards resolution. However, in the real world her trajectory is towards death, even if the film offers an alternate story in which she transforms and enters into a new equilibrium. Her actions, motivated by the Faun, propel her towards her actual end. Ofelia has moral choices in the film, as would her classic fairy story equivalents. She chooses to ignore the Faun's warning about not eating from the Pale Man's table and ultimately chooses the life of her brother over the possibility of total escape into the fantasy resolution offered by the Faun. Her lapses are justified in terms of her naivety and innocence and are not ambiguously motivated. *Pan's Labyrinth* thus sits within the rich and diverse genre of fairy tale influenced narratives that include Cocteau's *Beauty and the Beast* (1946), as well as Jim Henson's 1986 film *Labyrinth*.

GENRE

Genre study is the study of categorisation. It is a tool within film analysis that aids the student of film in their identification of the composite elements of a film text. Genre essentially means 'type', and within each type of film there are standard conventions. Within genres there are sub-genres that vary the use of conventions or mix them with those of other genres to create 'hybrid' genres (e.g. *Alien* (1979) might be considered a science fiction/horror hybrid). Genres of film can go in and out of fashion, they can become re-ignited because of the success of one particular film at the box office. There is often a financial motivation behind genres that dominate a particular period of cinema scheduling. Consider the current dominance of super hero films. The *Batman* and *Spider-Man* franchises have now been joined by *Iron Man* (2008) *Captain America* (2011, 2014) and *Thor* (2011, 2013), who have all joined forces in *The Avengers* (2012, 2015). The *Superman* franchise has its recent addition (*Man of Steel* (2013)) and the *X-Men* films not only have an initial trilogy, but individual characters, Wolverine being the first, are being given their own spin-offs. To what extent an initial concept can keep being plundered and still be an exciting and fertile channel is debatable. However, the truth is that prequels and sequels will continue to proliferate as long as the money keeps rolling in. Genre is, therefore, not only an analytical tool within Film Studies, but also a key factor within production (what to make?), distribution (is it a Memorial Weekend blockbuster or a late-autumn Oscar contender?) and exhibition (how many screens to show it on?) choices.

Del Toro has always been interested in the fantasy and horror genres. As a child his three favourite actors were Boris Karloff, Vincent Price and Peter Cushing, three actors with clear horror film credentials. Boris Karloff became the 'face' of Frankenstein's monster in the 1930s with *Frankenstein* (1931), *Bride of Frankenstein* (1935) and *Son of Frankenstein* (1939). Although Vincent Price did not begin his career in horror films, his shift to a horror focus in the 1950s produced *The House of Wax* (1953) and the (Gothic writer) Edgar Allen Poe inspired, *The House of Usher* (1960) and *The Pit and the Pendulum* (1961). Peter Cushing differed from Karloff and Price in that he did not make a name for himself playing the monster/creature. His association with the famous Hammer Horror production company saw him play Victor Frankenstein in the 1957 film *The Curse of Frankenstein* and Van Helsing, Dracula's nemesis, in the 1958 production *Dracula*.

Del Toro's fascination with the horror genre is clear:

' ... there is certainly a re-assurance to our well-being to be able to vicariously see the misfortune of someone else... The other power of the genre is that there is no other that generates images that stay embedded in your mind so strongly.' (del Toro in Wood , 2006)

It is not just the visual power of the horror genre that seems to attract del Toro, but also its use as an antidote to repression. Although horror films can be deeply conservative in their value systems ('slasher' films in particular, promote a world in which the sexually reticent tend to escape slaughter, whereas the promiscuous get butchered), they can also be progressive and liberating; especially when the alternate reality they construct acts as an antidote to the horrors of the real world. Ofelia's encounters with the fantasy horror characters within *Pan's Labyrinth* are nothing in comparison to her clashes with her monstrous step-father. The site of horror in classic horror films is an isolated place in which humanity is devalued and threat abounds. In this film, it is very clear which environment holds the most threat. The old Mill that the Fascists take over becomes a place of summary judgement, torture and death.

Pan's Labyrinth is a film in which visual elements are designed specifically to engage, shock and provoke. Early examples of the horror genre, such as Robert Wiene's *Das Cabinet des Dr. Caligari* (1920) and F.W. Murnau's *Nosferatu* (1922), were full of visual spectacle and although later examples of the genre often became less visually sophisticated, they were still intent on having a profound (physical) impact on their viewers. These early horror films presented light and dark in conflict and tension with each other. The real and fantasy worlds within *Pan's Labyrinth* also present a collision between light and dark. The real world of the Mill is a place of dark corners and shadows. It is inhospitable and lacking in comfort. In contrast, the fantasy settings are far more detailed and the court of the fantasy kingdom is especially light filled. The continuity in horror is that it places innocence in front of terror and demands that the audience enter fully into the threatening world that had been created. *Pan's Labyrinth* juxtaposes light and dark, both in terms of *mise-en-scène* and ideology. The grim reality of the Mill has a counterpoint in the fantasy world, especially in the imagined resolution to the fantasy narrative, in which the court of Ofelia's father is a stunning place of light,

The court of the fairy kingdom

sumptuous clothing and exaggerated iconography (the sky high thrones, in particular). The moribund nature of the Mill and, therefore, Fascism also finds its antidote in this scene, where Ofelia is free to live and take her rightful place in the fantasy kingdom.

A key atmospheric element within horror is the generation of foreboding and menace. The film language section of this study guide will explore this in more detail; however, it is important to mention it here as a factor within genre definition. Cinematography, *mise-en-scène*, sound and editing all contribute to the construction of a film's atmosphere. A sense of menace is essential within any successful horror film, as it infuses the viewing experience with a feeling of personal threat. If the audience does not suspend their disbelief, enter the world of the film and, in the case of horror, feel threatened by it, then the physical response demanded by the genre simply does not happen. It is not just Jamie Leigh Curtis's character that is menaced by Michael Myers in *Halloween* (John Carpenter, 1978), it is us. The effective manipulation of space and sound within her final confrontation with the 'monster' ultimately places us in the closet with her. We feel her claustrophobic terror and see Myers's relentless, apparently supernatural attack. Lighting choices are key in constructing a sense of foreboding in horror, for example, as are aural motifs and genre awareness. The audience's understanding of horror conventions makes them acutely aware that mists, fogs and shadows can 'contain things', or that a minor chord on the soundtrack can signal an attack. The two

The bleeding book

descending notes of John Williams's classic *Jaws* score, for example, signal threat, relentlessness and terror, almost on a primal level.

Ofelia's journey is full of menace. Her quests pit her against monsters, the bleeding book signals the terrible loss of her mother. She is seen crawling through tunnels, hiding under beds and climbing down into the labyrinth, in a visual representation of diminished and diminishing space. She is menaced on all levels; physically, emotionally, psychologically and, as representative of the innocence crushed by Fascism, ideologically.

Fantasy cinema, as with all other genres, has a clear set of conventions. Fantasy films are designed to engage the viewer through striking visuals. Their cinematic palette is rich and vibrant. *Pan's Labyrinth*'s 2006 Academy Awards for Cinematography and Art Direction are testament to its visual impact. The Mill is often dour or, by contrast, inferno-like. The labyrinth and the quest locations, however, are rich and visually varied. Within classic conventions, the arena of fantasy in a film is one where the rational has been rejected and the sub-conscious is made visually manifest. The unexpected becomes the norm and the fantasy elements become increasingly presented as real. The reality of the Faun and the labyrinth is never questioned by Ofelia. The viewer increasingly sees the fantasy characters and creatures within the context of the real world, in a blurring of fantasy and reality that is consistent with fantasy films.

Fantasy films use the supernatural, myth and legend to draw on for both characters and storylines and *Pan's Labyrinth* is no exception. The myth of the labyrinth is straight from Greek mythology. Daedalus created the labyrinth at Knossos for King Minos of Crete. Its function was to hold the Minotaur (half-man, half-bull), which was eventually killed by the Athenian, Theseus. The only way that Theseus could then escape from the labyrinth was with the help of Ariadne, who gave him a ball of string to tie at the start of the labyrinth, unravel as he went in and thus secure a path out. Labyrinths are different from mazes, in terms of their accessibility. Mazes have multiple possible paths, they are ambiguous. Labyrinths on the other hand traditionally have one path, albeit convoluted. They are unambiguous and lead those in them back to the beginning again, hopefully having gained greater insight into their predicament. As a metaphor, a labyrinth is a means by which greater understanding can be gained. The labyrinth within del Toro's film always leads Ofelia to its centre. It opens an extra path to help her beat Vidal to the centre at the climax of the film. It has a monster at its core. Del Toro describes the labyrinth thus:

> **'A maze is a place where you get lost... But a labyrinth is essentially a place of transit, an ethical, moral transit to an inevitable centre.'**
> (del Toro in Kermode, *The Guardian*, 5 November 2006)

The other side of the labyrinth, for Ofelia, is death, but the other side for the resistance is the destruction of Vidal, the symbol of Fascism in the narrative.

Pan's Labyrinth also uses characters from mythology. Although the English translation of the Spanish is 'Pan', the original is *El Laberinto del Fauno* ('The Faun's Labyrinth'). Fauns exist within Roman mythology as spirits of the woodland. They have the body of a man, but the horns, tail, ears and legs of a goat. Del Toro's Faun is formed from trees, leaves and wood. It is half-man, half-goat, sharing the explicit connection to nature of the Roman original. Mythical, supernatural and legendary locations and characters are used for a number of reasons in fantasy films. They promote an unreality and lack of rationality that then allows fantastical events to happen. They offer universally understood storylines and universally recognised iconography to the viewer and reject cultural specificity. They represent the workings of the sub-conscious. *Pan's*

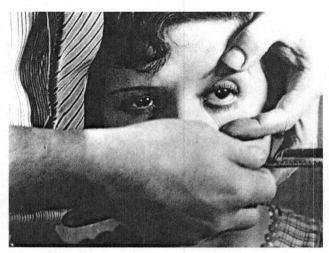

Un chien adalou

Labyrinth is essentially a story about good versus evil. Although it does have a specific historical backdrop, the story of the child's battle with the horrors of the adult world is one that has universal appeal.

It is the attempt to represent the sub-conscious visually that links fantasy films to Surrealist examples. Both movements use stunning or shocking visuals to attempt to represent the human psyche and what happens to it when repressed. Whereas early Surrealist films, such as *Un chien andalou* (Buñuel, 1929) took a more Freudian stance, offering a visual discussion of the consequence of sexual repression, fantasy films do not tend to be driven by Freudian discourse. In *Un chien andalou* the brutal initial image of an eyeball being slit is a clear indication of what the sub-conscious can generate when repressed. Likewise in Buñuel's 1930 film *L'Âge d'or*, the female protagonist sucks the toe of a statue when she is denied sexual expression with the object of her desire. Although *Pan's Labyrinth* is not an investigation into the psycho-sexual world of its main character, nor about sexual repression, it is still about the power of the imagination and the workings of the sub-conscious; something that it (and other fantasy cinema) does share with Surrealism. Surrealist cinema is also political and in this way shares characteristics with del Toro's brand of fantasy cinema. Both of the aforementioned Surrealist films have clear targets. Buñuel's Surrealist piece, *The Phantom of Liberty* (1974), although much later, takes on the mantel of *Un chien andalou* and *L'Âge d'or* in its scathing attacks on institutions such as the clergy, the judiciary and the military. *Pan's Labyrinth* uses its stunning fantasy world as an antidote to the political repression of Fascism, just as it uses it as a means by which to discuss Ofelia's desperate emotional and psychological plight.

Pan's Labyrinth is thus a film that draws from two distinctive genre pools and conflates conventions in a powerfully original way. It acknowledges its genre heritage and then takes the viewer on a unique journey. In some ways the viewer's quest is as complex and difficult as Ofelia's. We are charged with the task of unravelling the complex visual, thematic and narrative enigmas of the film, of understating the national, moral, physical and psychological impact of Fascism and, perhaps the biggest task of all, of accepting the death of the child at the end of the narrative, a resolution that is unquestionably challenging.

MESSAGES AND VALUES

The answer to the question of what any film is 'about' will receive a plural answer. A film may profess to be 'about' an idea or event, but will invariably discuss other issues, too. When discussing the messages and values of a film it is important to remain open to both a film's potentially shifting focus and to one's own response to it. The film student should not disregard what a film or its director might say that it is about, but should place this 'reading' in a context with other 'readings'. It is essential that challenge is brought to any critical assessment of a film and this challenge should be of our own interpretations as well as those of others. The analysis of messages and values within a film text is a process of considering the constituent elements of that film. Messages and values are constructed through the textual elements of a film. They are supported and confirmed by *mise-en-scène*, cinematography, editing and sound. Messages and values are subjective in the sense that they only really exist if the viewer realises that they are there. This is why informed and well-substantiated personal voice is an essential part of any effective piece of film analysis. This section will offer one interpretation of the messages and values of *Pan's Labyrinth*.

The way in which oppression is represented in this film is that it can be ideological, emotional and psychological. Before the Fascists came to power, Spain (according to the film) was child-like in its freedom from oppressive ideology. Themes of oppression and resistance run through this film, in both the fantasy and the real narratives. The pre-narrative to *Pan's Labyrinth* has seen the Fascists occupy the rural community in order to try and put down the resistance. The Mill, a symbol of the previous life of the community, has become an outpost. Once a productive part of that community, it is now still. The people's food is rationed and the resistance hunted in a clear representation of Fascist oppression. The *mise-en-scène* of the Mill, its darkness and shadows, clearly signify the political signatures of its new inhabitants. The iconography of the lock and key, under which Vidal holds provisions that should belong to the people, also reflects the enforced 'rule' of the Fascists. These are but two of the many textual elements that substantiate the connections made in the film between Fascism and oppression.

The cruel fascist Vidal in full uniform

What is oppressed and what is resisted in *Pan's Labyrinth* is more than ideological, however; it is psychological and emotional, too. Ofelia resists the will of Vidal through her imagination and her conscience; she resists giving up her brother and sacrifices herself instead. Although Vidal continues to dominate any frame in which he is placed with Ofelia, when they are in their different worlds, Ofelia's props often act to counter-balance Vidal's and represent her lack of conformity. She destroys her 'uniform', the dress that her mother Carmen expects her to wear for Vidal. The destruction might not be intentional, but Ofelia transgresses the moment she takes it off. Vidal is continually seen buttoned up tight in his uniform. His grooming is almost fetishistic and connotes his subservience to rule and order. Both Vidal and Ofelia are seen with keys, but whereas Vidal's key is used to control, hide and oppress, Ofelia's prop allows her to liberate the knife from the Pale Man's lair and continue with her quest.

Carmen's passivity with Vidal is in contrast to Ofelia's. Carmen gives up personal control and allows herself to be oppressed because of her own needs and the socio-economic position that she perceives a woman like her to be in. Carmen acquiesces to Vidal when he wants her to use the wheelchair, a piece of iconography that represents a taking away of mobility and freedom. She allows herself to be silenced by Vidal at the dinner party and embarrassed when he calls her account of the beginning of their relationship 'silly stories'.

Ofelia and Carmen

The representation of the family in *Pan's Labyrinth* is another key area for discussion. The family is restorative and restored in this film, but only within the fantasy narrative. When Ofelia enters the light-soaked fairy kingdom, she sees her family restored. They are not only alive again, but are royal and adored by their many subjects. Ofelia's quest has ended and she has been reunited with her family, as well as re-instated to her birthright. The *mise-en-scène* and cinematography of this scene both point to its credentials as a resolution. However, in the real world of the film, family is a much more fraught notion. In the real world families are destroyed and lost. The family unit is utterly vulnerable and its sanctuary cannot be guaranteed. As a support for individuals when facing oppression, the family does not always overcome. It is significant, for example, that the rabbit poachers are father and son, and that the father is forced to watch the brutalising of the son by Vidal. Ofelia's mother is no armour for Ofelia against Vidal. However, in the case of Mercedes and her brother, the strength of the family does eventually save the day. Families in *Pan's Labyrinth* are mostly broken, missing members or, in the case of the step-family, cold and bullying. They can be surrogate and Mercedes does become a surrogate mother for Ofelia. However, Mercedes cannot save Ofelia from Vidal. Resistance to a dominant and oppressive ideology requires whole communities the film seems to be suggesting, and not just the family.

Discussions of gender within *Pan's Labyrinth* are presented through three groups of characters: women, men and the creatures. The three main female characters are Ofelia, Carmen and Mercedes. In many ways, Ofelia is far closer in her representation to Mercedes than to her mother. As has already been stated, Carmen is a passive character, who needs Vidal in order to define and financially support her. She gives up her freedom and potentially that of her daughter's in order to secure that support. Ofelia describes her mother as 'pretty' to Mercedes and 'beautiful' to her unborn brother. In terms of her role in a gender politics debate, Carmen is represented as subject and subjective. She is there to be looked at, to produce children and to obey. Mercedes, in contrast, resists. She is active in the resistance movement and smuggles supplies to them. Mercedes represents a female spirit that is far more indomitable than Carmen's. She is courageous and can inflict great violence on her oppressors; the half-smile that she carves into Vidal's face is brutal and grotesque. Ofelia also resists oppression. She is transgressive and fights for what she believes to be true. Ofelia does not have Mercedes' capacity for violence, but then she is still a child. These three female characters provide a discussion of the varying responses that women have when faced with crisis.

Mercedes and Ofelia

The male characters in the film are not so much shades of each other as opposites. There are many patterns of diametrical opposition in *Pan's Labyrinth* and the gender debate in the film is no different. The ideology of Vidal and his men is in direct contrast to that of the resistance movement (who, apart from Mercedes, are all men). The two groups of men occupy very different environments in the film. The *mise-en-scène* of the forest presents a vitality and potency that is not evident in the Mill. The forest is green and open, as opposed to dark and confined. The Fascists wear uniforms, the resistance do not. The hierarchy of the Fascists is clear and fixed, whereas there seems to be more democracy with the men of the resistance. Dr Ferreiro is a man whose humility and dignity are evident from the start, in common with the character of the orphanage physician, Casares, in *The Devil's Backbone*. He is not without fear, but continues to aid the resistance. When framed with Vidal, Ferreiro is smaller and less rigid in his posture, but he is the character who directly admonishes Vidal for his subservience to ideology. Vidal is, of course, the main male character and monster of the film. His masculinity is cold, brutal and demanding of acknowledgement. Vidal's sense of himself as a potent male is so strong that he refuses to believe that his baby will be anything other than male. When Ferreiro asks him why he is so sure of the unborn child's gender, Vidal replies 'Don't fuck with me'. For Vidal, his sense of himself as one in a long line of men is essential. He wants his legacy to live on through his son, but thankfully the viewer knows that this will not happen. Vidal is Fascism distilled, he is also the monster that lurks at the back of every child's psyche. Unlike the men of the resistance or Dr Ferreiro, Vidal has no sense of empathy or sympathy for other individuals. He is the juggernaut of Fascism personified.

The creatures within the fantasy narrative are in some ways genderless. Although the viewer might assume a gender for them, it is perhaps in their more abstract associations that the creatures are particularly interesting. As physical manifestations of primal fears, the creatures do not need to be gender identified. They are greed, brutality, death, disease and age. They represent humankind's worst fears for themselves, but they also contribute to the ideological debate through their need to control and destroy. The Pale Man and the Faun do not have the primary sexual characteristics of men, but then neither do they have the primary sexual characteristics of women. The *assumption* is that they are male, but this has as much to do with their words and actions as it does with their appearance. Both the Pale Man and the Faun can be read as representing a type of masculinity that is in conflict with femininity, rather than in harmony with it, and thus, they share the threatening masculinity that is evident in Vidal. The Pale Man is relentless in his attempt to capture Ofelia. His violence is sudden and horrific, when his environment is under threat. Vidal shares both of these characteristics. The Faun is controlling, ambiguous and even cruel. It displays none of the maternal care and warmth that has been associated with female characters in the film.

The theme of childhood has been explored by del Toro before in *The Devil's Backbone*, and *Pan's Labyrinth* acts as further exploration of what it is to be a child, especially one living in a grim reality. As has been discussed previously, the position of the (often female) child within the classic fairy story narrative is one of abandonment or loss, of peril and subsequently of growth. Typically, the pre-pubescent girl will confront increasingly dangerous challenges and overcome them, in order to regain her rightful place in the world and enter maturity. This child is pitched against danger in order to present a clash between innocence and evil and it is this diametric opposition that renders fairy tales essentially shocking.

In childhood the power of the imagination is at its strongest and thus can be used as a weapon against hurt and pain. The imagination acts to filter pain through images that are tangible. The potential understanding that the imagination can bring to a child is through the externalisation of evil; a 'giving shape' to fears and allowing the child to stand in front of them and confront them. In *Pan's Labyrinth*, Ofelia's childhood is already blighted by the loss of her father and her uprooting from her previous home. Her world gradually diminishes, to the point where both her parents are dead and it is at this point that the film presents childhood as at its most vulnerable. Ofelia takes solace from her stories and uses the fantasy world that she imagines to counter the horrors within the real world. The universe of childhood in this film is presented as lonely and vulnerable. Ofelia is introverted and scared, and the only way she can escape the present is to construct a fantasy world in which she has the chance to be re-united with her family. In order to present the atrocities and oppression of the real world more starkly, del Toro shows the direct effects of it on a child and these effects are indeed terrible. This is a film about moral choices and it is Ofelia's eventual self-sacrifice that highlights the lack of morality of the Fascists. Childhood might be a time of vulnerability and questioning, but it is also presented by *Pan's Labyrinth* as a period during which instinctive choices are key. Childhood should be an unfettered and unpolluted time, before life's disappointments, hardships and brutalities can take their toll and the power to imagine may be lost. If it becomes a period of loss and pain, then a great crime has been committed. What Ofelia is forced to experience is a direct consequence of the mistakes made in the adult world.

Death and rebirth are also key themes within *Pan's Labyrinth*. There are literal and figurative deaths within the film. Carmen, Dr Ferreiro, Ofelia and Vidal all die, but it is only Ofelia's death that is presented as transformative. Carmen's death is during childbirth. It has been predicted both by her worsening physical state and by the viewer's understanding that the character of Ofelia must be left entirely alone in order to reach the ultimate low that will hopefully stimulate her fight back. Ferreiro's death is a consequence of his transgression against the will of Vidal and thus is a testament to the latter's barbarity and cowardice. Vidal's own death seems to surprise him, as he assumes that he will be able to die having confirmed his legacy. He is denied this and dies knowing that he will not have a future in the memory of his son. Ofelia's death is self-sacrificial and the presentation of her subsequent 'life' in the fantasy narrative codes it as necessary. She is visually and thematically re-born at the end of the film. In the reality of the film's diegesis, the rebirth represents the resistance movement's hopes.

FILM LANGUAGE

Mise-en-scène

Mise-en-scène is a French phrase that best translates in English as 'put into the scene'. This includes setting, décor, costume, props, body language and make-up. As with all other textual elements, *mise-en-scène* conveys meaning and this includes information concerning character emotion, psychological state, mood, atmosphere, historical time, genre and point in the narrative.

In some films the *mise-en-scène* dominates, as they are constructed as cinematic tableau, i.e. a series of pictures or paintings. Peter Webber's 2003 film *Girl with a Pearl Earring*, for example, is about painting and the emotional process of creation and is thus shot as such: eye-level, long and mid shots are frequently combined with specifically placed props in order to approximate Vermeer's work and make the viewer feel that they are staring straight at a canvas. The film presents a series of scenes in which the setting and props evoke the historical period of Vermeer's work, as well as approximating the work itself. *Mise-en-scène* can also act as a visual representation of a damaged and perverse psychological state. The taxidermy within Norman Bates' office in Hitchcock's *Psycho* (1960) presents not only Norman's stultified mind, but also the ominous and threatening world that Marion Crane has entered.

Lists of conventions within genre films always include *mise-en-scène*. Action films include props that immediately denote the genre: weapons, cars, boats, planes and other types of technology that can be associated with excitement and adrenaline. The setting of science fiction films is space, other planets, and dystopian or utopian representations of future Earth. Any attempt to 'read' narrative can also be helped by analysis of *mise-en-scène*. States of new equilibrium or resolution tend to have elements of *mise-en-scène* that signal them as such. The final scene in Steven Spielberg's 2002 film *Minority Report*, for example, still presents a scarred world, but one in which Tom Cruise's character, previously estranged from his wife following the disappearance of their son, can look forward to a future. The pregnant state of his wife and the fact that they occupy the same space again is testament to the state of new equilibrium.

Costume and make-up are also key elements within *mise-en-scène* and can be as potentially evocative as the other elements. Costume is an important mechanism through which historical period can be signalled, for example. Costume is also key within representational debates regarding the socio-economic or cultural position of groups or individuals. If costume elements change within the course of a narrative, this can create key meaning regarding a character's position or state of mind. When Geena Davis's housewife character morphs into her previous self ('Charly', the crack assassin) in Renny Harlin's film *The Long Kiss Goodnight* (1996), her newly peroxide, shorn locks and black clothes present a new stage in the narrative in which she will truly fight back. Charly's thick kohl eye-liner and increased make-up also represent the more sexually provocative elements of her character.

There is an immediacy to *mise-en-scène* that makes it different from other micro elements. The viewer can see it and will react instinctively to the worlds being created. The *mise-en-scène* of del Toro's film is immediately absorbing. It challenges the viewer in a number of ways: to find comparisons and contrasts between the two worlds; to suspend disbelief even within the fantasy setting, and to immerse him/herself within these worlds, frightening as they evidently are.

Del Toro's visual influences included paintings and illustrations. The fairy tale illustrations of Arthur Rackham, for example, were highly influential. Del Toro said of Rackham's work:

'There is a perverse undercurrent in his work. His vision was plagued by knotty, twisted things that had a perverse will to live.' (www.panslabyrinth.com)

A Rackham illustration for Alice's Adventures in Wonderland circa 1907

Del Toro's vision of the world of *Pan's Labyrinth* is one in which there are clear parallels between the real world characters and sets and the imaginary ones. The film gives centre stage to the power of the imagination and the need to retain imagination in order to counter-point the horrors of the real world.

There is no doubt that *Pan's Labyrinth* is a very beautiful-looking film. Its visual elements have been universally applauded both by critics and audiences. In order to consider elements of *mise-en-scène* in the film more closely, this section will use three headings to distinguish between different sections of the film: Fantasy, Fantasy meets Reality, and Reality. This is not to say that there are not more crossovers than this, but in terms of *mise-en-scène* the distinction is useful. This section is also presented with the acknowledgement that in one sense (i.e. it's a work of fiction, not a documentary) none of the film is real and all of it is fantasy.

Fantasy

Although the opening images of Ofelia would seem to place her in the real world of the film, there are elements of the *mise-en-scène* that immediately position her in the fantasy narrative. Ofelia's hand is caked in blood, which drips from her nose. The blood coming from her nose then starts to reverse and the fantasy narrative is signalled. The colour of the blood contrasts strongly with the dark, hard stone and it is absolutely clear that this child is in dire peril. Ofelia's eye is then used as a kind of portal, into both the fantasy kingdom and the past of the film's narrative. The power of the visual is clearly signified with the eye and through it we see a subjective world. The fantasy kingdom is introduced as a place cut into rocks, as if it is an integral part of the Earth. The spires, turrets and vaulted roofs of the kingdom are evidence of its grandeur. It has the same kind of blue-grey hue as the other fantasy settings within the film and has doorways guarded by sphinx-like creatures, which reinforce the gravitas of the place. The spiralling steps that Ofelia is seen running up support the fantasy and fairy tale credentials of the scene. The kingdom is enigmatic, it is other-worldly. It is neither a benevolent or an ominous setting at this point, but the mist over the buildings, coupled with the magisterial architecture make this place both fascinating and somewhat unsettling.

Ofelia's relationship with fairy stories and fantasy narratives includes being the creator of them, too. The story she tells her unborn brother is accompanied by an incredibly striking image. The magic rose of the story is blue and is set against a blood red sky (still an echo of the amniotic blood seen before the edit). The rose's seeming unnaturalness is coded by Ofelia's voice-over as pure. It is threatened by the vicious thorns of the vines that grow around the mountain. The thorns are full of poison and stop the rose from ever being able 'to bequeath its gift to anyone'. The rose is beautiful, unattainable and gradually being destroyed by the invading thorns. This story is told by Ofelia and her pain and fear are clear within the narrative of the rose. However, the story could equally concern Ofelia's own mother or Spain itself. The story of the rose does two things. It establishes the close connection between Ofelia and the fantasy world; and quickly establishes the ideological connotations within the fantasy elements of the film.

The eponymous setting of the film is a powerful creation. As stated in the Genre section of this guide, labyrinths have one route to their centre and then back to their beginning. The journey through a labyrinth is one of enlightenment. Del Toro's labyrinth is dark and gloomy, and at its core are steps descending downwards. At the centre of this 'inner sanctum' are a series of decreasing circles with a totem-like structure at the centre. The images on this totem are explained later to Ofelia as representing herself and the Faun. The labyrinth is presented as magical and as an escape for Ofelia from the world of the Mill. Like the Faun, it is ambiguous, however, and the *mise-en-scène* substantiates this ambiguity. The labyrinth might contain information, stories and hope; but it is dark, dank and full of shadows. The Faun has the body of a man, the legs of a goat and its skin is covered in twigs and leaves. At another point in the film, it is seen tearing off pieces of meat with its teeth from a lump in its hand. The Faun is recognisable and yet not, frightening at times and yet comforting at others. The Faun's own *mise-en-scène* is as ambiguous as the other micro elements used to present it.

On Ofelia's first meeting with the Faun, it gives her 'The Book of Crossroads'. This is a large, beautifully bound tomb; absolutely the stuff of fairy stories. The book is initially blank, implying some control that Ofelia might have over events. After all, if she can write her own story, can't she control her trajectory and the imagery that surround it? This piece of

Ofelia and The Book of Crossroads

iconography, however, contains messages that are gradually revealed. The book shows Ofelia the tree that is to be her next fantasy setting. The roots of this tree are being destroyed. It is literally being eaten alive. The links being made between Spain and the tree are clear. It is at this point in the narrative that Ofelia reveals her crescent moon birthmark; described as a mark of true ancestry by the Faun, both Ofelia and the viewer are guided into a reading of this birthmark as an indication of her true heritage.

As with the tradition of fairy stories (discussed previously in the Genre section), the 'Princess'/heroine character has to transgress in order to complete her journey. Within this first quest, Ofelia must take off the dress her mother has painstakingly created for her and leave it on the tree's branches, only to return to find it muddied and ruined. If we 'read' the dress as representative of the mother's attempts to encourage Ofelia to bend to the Captain's rules, then its destruction and 'shedding' are absolutely necessary within the narrative. It is interesting, however, that the dress is forest green. This links Ofelia to nature, to the Faun and therefore to the fantasy narrative, rather than the narrative in which the Fascists exist. The dress also links Ofelia to the character of Alice in *Alice in Wonderland*: both Ofelia and Alice embark on quests; both descend into unknown worlds, populated by weird and wonderful characters; and both are female children on the brink of puberty. When Ofelia eventually encounters the Toad, it is not just its size that is monstrous. Its greedy devouring of bugs and slimy skin are revolting enough, but it is the Toad's spewing out of its own stomach that creates particularly repellent *mise-en-scène*. The Toad is not terrifying; it is more of a grotesque character that represents the greed of an unwelcome and invading ideology. Ofelia finds another piece of classic fairy story iconography – a key – in the Toad's stomach, proving that out of any revolting circumstance, something useful might come.

The lair of the Pale Man is an extraordinary place of childhood (and adult, for that matter) nightmares. The corridor to his banquet room is vaulted, gothic and not without some grandeur. The *mise-en-scène* of the entrance hall does not suggest the abode of a squalid character, but rather one of some status. Ofelia's journey into the realm of the Pale Man is timed with an hourglass, a classic symbol of the race against time that is often used as a structural device within fairy stories and fantasy narratives. The banquet room of the Pale Man is a shrine to greed and excess. The huge table is spread with blood red jellies and fruit. The wine is red, too, and all of these elements serve to contrast with the bloodless Pale Man. The iconography of the lair becomes even more terrifying when Ofelia looks up and sees a series of paintings depicting the Pale Man's slaughter of children. The place is indeed a shrine to his own barbarity. There is a roaring fire in the hearth in this room. It is as if every comfort were there but not as comfort for the Pale Man, more a lure to his victims. The Pale Man's actions have meant that he can no longer access normal nourishment or warmth. In one of the most horrific images of the whole film, Ofelia then sees a pile of children's shoes. Reminiscent of the piles of shoes found by the Allied forces on the liberation of the extermination camps after WWII, this image absolutely sums up the role of the Pale Man. He is the monster of the fairy tale, the Bogey Man lurking at the back of a child's psyche and the destroyer of innocence (whether this is a state of individual childhood or a whole nation). The Pale Man's visual monstrousness is constructed meticulously. His face is molten skin and he has to place eyes in his hands to see. His skin hangs from him and his legs are emaciated, indicating his inherent lifelessness. The Pale Man's body language is at once elderly and bestial. His *mise-en-scène* seems inspired by the Cronos figure from Greek mythology; a father who devoured his children in an, ultimately unsuccessful, attempt to stop them usurping his position. As the Pale Man picks fairies out of the air and bites off their heads, pulling strings of blood and skin between their bodies

The Pale Man at his table

and their heads, he is further confirmed as being part of the horror genre tradition.

As has been discussed in previous sections, the last scenes of *Pan's Labyrinth* are not quite as simple as they might initially seem. The fantasy kingdom that the viewer encountered in the opening minutes of the film is returned to in the last scene. The *mise-en-scène* has changed, however, and it has done so in accordance with the film's presentation of fantasy as ultimately liberating. Ofelia enters the fantasy kingdom at the end of the film in a haze of fairy particles. She looks at her hands, which are now clean of blood, and in this one movement, the film presents the viewer with a scene in which escape to the fantasy world has followed Ofelia's death. If Ofelia is cognisant of having been 'saved' then the viewer should take some solace from that, too. Ofelia is transformed. Her clothes are rich fabrics of stunning colour and her rightful place is a beautiful throne on top of a magisterial column. The court she has entered is sun-filled and golden. The fairies are alive, as are Ofelia's family. This scene could be read as an attempt to dilute the viewer's horror over the shooting of a child, through the beauty and grandeur of the fantasy *mise-en-scène* and establishing a forward movement to the narrative. It could also purely be read as a resolution to the fantasy narrative and not to the reality of events.

Fantasy meets Reality

In a film that does not draw a distinct line between imagination and reality, it is to be expected that the distinction between real and fantasy visuals should be blurred, too. Whether this blurring accelerates at a pace commensurate with Ofelia's growing misery or it happens more and more to draw in the viewer, or a mixture of both, the fantasy and real world in *Pan's Labyrinth* become closer as the film progresses. Ofelia's initial meeting with the fantasy world comes very early in the film when she gets out of the car and finds a rock on the ground. Ofelia's world is already in jeopardy and she is ready to escape. The stone is in fact a fragment of a statue; it is the eye of the statue. Ofelia replaces the eye and in doing so completes the statue. As a piece of iconography, the stone eye is a key to unlock the fairy world and a symbol of the need to look more closely at the world around us. Once the eye is replaced Ofelia sees the unusual insect for the first time. The power of the child in the fairy tale and the need for the imagination when the psyche is under duress are clear messages presented within this sequence.

'The Book of Crossroads' has already been mentioned in the previous Fantasy section, but is actually an example of a fantastical element that seems to exist (at least for Ofelia) in the real world, too. Although the book is first used as a traditional fairy tale prop, i.e. it outlines details of a task for the central protagonist, the second time Ofelia consults it its predictions are truly terrible. Whereas Ofelia's first look into the book shows her a children's story image of a tree and beautiful monastic manuscript-style text, her second consultation reveals an image of ovaries, a womb and blood that predicts her mother's near miscarriage. This second prediction brings the pain of the real world crashing into the (so far) safe world of the Faun, the labyrinth and the quests.

The Faun enters Ofelia's bedroom on three occasions. Its presence signals her increasing separation from the real world and her need to throw herself into fantasy. The Faun's presence in Ofelia's bedroom is the stuff of childhood nightmares; the monster who can always get in and arrives whenever it wants, but also the potential liberator who can give the child the means to escape. On the first visit, the Faun gives Ofelia the Mandrake 'baby', a grotesque approximation of a human child. The 'baby' is half-foetus, half-vegetable and needs to be fed on blood, a vampiric tendency that codes it as monstrous. As a metaphor, the Mandrake 'baby' could be read in many ways. It is a succubus that needs human sacrifice to survive, i.e. a political system that becomes harder and harder to feed. However, the positive impact of the root on Ofelia's mother can't be denied and thus it might signify the need to utilise all means, no matter how initially repellent, to survive. When Vidal discovers the root and Ofelia's mother throws it into the fire, Ofelia's hopes are symbolically burnt with it.

The Faun's second visit to Ofelia is far more fraught. Ofelia has transgressed in the lair of the Pale Man and two of the Faun's fairies have been killed. In this scene, the Faun dominates its environment even more so than before. It seems to take up more physical space in the room, its body language indicates fury, and when it turns, bends and disappears into shadows, it is as if Ofelia's hopes of escape have disappeared with it. The Faun's third visit to the real world is after Ofelia's mother's death and its body language is completely different. It is comforting, almost paternal and re-establishes the quests that Ofelia feels might give her final release.

The concluding image of the film appears like a final statement on the discussions about the role of fantasy within reality that have existed in *Pan's Labyrinth*. The final image is one of a flower opening. The flower symbolises hope, rejuvenation and life, but the voice-over that accompanies it also adds comment to the debate. The flower, by extension the world of the imagination and by further extension, one type of truth, is 'visible only to those who know where to look'. Whether the 'looking' is done by Ofelia, children, the film viewer or someone with a particular ideological stance, the message seems to be about the need to strive and to believe. This might seem a strange message when the central protagonist of the film, who believed and strived, is not ultimately saved by the imagination; but criticism of this nature would imply that the film had, at one point, suggested that the imagination could save an individual from the brutalities of life. The statement *Pan's Labyrinth* seems to be making is that the imagination can provide an escape from real life crisis, but will never overcome it.

Reality

The iconography related to Vidal is almost relentlessly brutal. Whether it is his father's watch that marks the exact point of his father's death, the razors with which he ceremoniously shaves himself or the guns he uses to dispatch farmers and resistance members alike, these props are all associated with violence, repression and oppression. He keeps the barn under lock and key. He forces his wife to use a wheelchair. The most obvious indictment of Vidal as both war criminal and monster is the scene in the barn where he tortures the stuttering resistance fighter. The barn had previously been a place where the Fascists hoarded supplies and rationed them to the impoverished rural community. Once the resistance has liberated these supplies, Vidal's revenge includes using the barn as a torture chamber. Vidal's body language is as controlled as ever in this scene. He smokes a cigarette and taunts the prisoner. Then in a horrific display of sadistic intent, Vidal presents his captive with the instruments that will be used to torture him. These props, the hammer, the pliers and the bradawl, are unveiled as an indication of the escalating pain that will be inflicted. Once the torture has been inflicted (off-screen) the body of the stuttering man is revealed as a brutalised canvas. His hand is deformed, broken and swollen. He has saliva dripping from his mouth and seems almost blinded. Vidal's impact on the bodies and minds of those who come into contact with him is devastating. It is presented by the film as suitable revenge, therefore, when Mercedes attacks Vidal in her bid for escape. She stabs him with the knife she is seen using to chop vegetables in previous scenes. This is a prop, therefore, that once symbolised Mercedes' enforced domestic servitude and is then used to release her from it. Mercedes slits Vidal's face into a bizarre, lop-sided grin. Like Batman's nemesis the Joker, Vidal has the happiness he destroys in others literally carved onto his face as a grim reminder of his actions and an ironic representation of his state of mind.

Costume is another carefully considered aspect of *mise-en-scène* in *Pan's Labyrinth*. Vidal's pristine uniform and shined shoes echo his rigidity of purpose. Ofelia's *Alice in Wonderland*-like, forest green dress has been discussed previously. Ofelia's mother's costume changes in the film are a gradual divestment of clothing. She is first seen in a dress, hat and coat. Her hair is neat and her make-up is carefully applied. As she becomes more subject to the will of Vidal and the demands of her difficult pregnancy, Carmen is stripped of not only her clothing, but also her dignity and her life. The clothing of the resistance members is a visual counter-balance to that of the Fascists. They do not have uniforms and, by extension, do not have the blind submission to power and ideology that a uniform implies in this film. The props and settings attached to the resistance are also completely different from those of the Fascists. The resistance hide in the woods. They seem part of it and dissolve in and out of the trees in a way that implies a real understanding of, and connection to, their environment. They have guns, rather than knives and their use of these guns is coded as justifiable in the film, as they invariably either kill to protect themselves or destroy the oppressive regime of the Fascists.

Camerawork

Camerawork can essentially be broken down into three discrete areas: camera distance, camera movement and camera angle. Framing and blocking also come into any discussion of the use of camera and for the purposes of this study guide, lighting will also be discussed in this section. Analysis of camera distance involves the study of how far the camera is away from its subject and what meanings the choice of distance might generate. Extreme long shots are generally used as establishing shots, for example, and extreme close-ups are often unsettling and synonymous with the thriller or horror genres. Consider the extreme close-ups of the 'final girl's' eye in Tobe Hooper's 1974 shocker *The Texas Chain Saw Massacre*, for example. The prolonged proximity is quite unbearable. Camera movement discussions include the study of panning, tilting, tracking and hand-held cinematography; 360 degree point-of-view pans, for example, can effectively place the viewer in the shoes of a panicked character, looking around for the source of threat. An upward tilt of the camera, such as the one used to introduce the character of Trip Fontaine, in Sofia Coppola's 1999 film, *The Virgin Suicides*, is immediately desirous of, and objectifying of, its subject.

The category of camera angles includes not only low and high, but also canted. The objectification or submission implied by a high or low angle is a common device in films to make meaning clear. Characters look up at creatures, the sky and buildings and this low angle shot implies an unequal status between observer and subject. Ofelia looks up at the Faun, for example, using a low angle to imply his status as potential threat. Canted (or Dutch) angles, which tilt the head of the camera 45 degrees, often imply disturbance to the narrative. When the character of Esteban dies, for example, in Pedro Almodovar's *All about my Mother* (1999), the viewer is positioned in Esteban's point-of-view. His head is lifted from the floor by his mother and the viewer, as Esteban, sees his mother's distraught face, through a canted angle.

Framing and blocking choices are other fertile areas for cinematic analysis. What or who dominates the frame has meaning, as does what or who is absent from it. Frames can be crowded, empty or move from crowded to empty. When the character of Lester Burnham first sees Angela (the object of his desire) at the basketball match in Sam Mendes's *American Beauty* (1999), he is framed amidst a sea of people. As his fantasy about her intensifies, his frame empties to leave just him, mesmerised by the cheerleader. Lighting choices can be evocative of genre. Chiaroscuro lighting (an extreme contrast between light and dark), for example, is a technical convention within *film noir*. Lighting can evoke mood and distinguish certain character roles. Lit from below, most normal-looking individuals take on an eerie countenance, let alone when a vampire or other monster is lit in this way.

The opening shot in *Pan's Labyrinth* is a pan across the screen, from right to left, of Ofelia. This counter-intuitive direction, coupled with the realisation that the pan is in fact up towards Ofelia (the viewer realises this when the camera turns 90 degrees to reveal the Ofelia is lying on the ground) immediately tells us that something is very wrong. Of course, the blood oozing from Ofelia's nose confirms this reaction. The camerawork in *Pan's Labyrinth* is very fluid, and evokes the dream-like fairy tale quality of the fantasy narrative and the unfettered movement of the imagination. After a zoom through Ofelia's eye, the camera then continues to pan across the fantasy kingdom, through an arch-way and then upwards, following Ofelia as she climbs a spiral stone staircase towards the light. This light then intensifies and dominates the screen. The implication of this light and the voice-over that accompanies it is that there is release and escape in the real world; however, the next crane shot that swoops through the debris of a once impressive building, immediately contradicts this promise of escape and hope. The next shot, a close-up of one of Ofelia's fairy stories, introduces the stories that she will use as a means of counter-balancing the horrors of war.

In the car, Ofelia and her mother are framed together. The mother is positioned in the left hand side of the frame and occupies more space. At this stage of the narrative, Ofelia and her mother are in unity, and Carmen is still implied to have some degree of strength. It is interesting that when Carmen meets Vidal, they are presented in a two-shot. Although often used to indicate a close relationship between two characters, the two-shot between Vidal and Carmen only serves to highlight their distance. Vidal initially leans in to whisper something to his wife and the viewer might hope for some tender words for the un-well Carmen. However what Vidal actually says is 'do it for me', i.e. use the wheelchair. Carmen has said 'no' and the viewer assumes that she wants to retain some independence, but this is quickly crushed by Vidal. The two-shot, therefore, rather than presenting a tender and close relationship between Vidal and Carmen, does the opposite. For the rest of their scenes together (which are not frequent), Vidal and Carmen are barely even in the same shot. This first meeting also establishes the relationship between Ofelia and Vidal. The over the shoulder low angle shot from behind Ofelia of Vidal, straight away infers his dominant nature.

As our narrative guide, Ofelia is to be followed and watched, and the camerawork within *Pan's Labyrinth* confirms this. As Ofelia first approaches the labyrinth, pans and tracks take the viewer on the same journey. A point-of-view shot then positions the viewer as Ofelia, looking up at the arch above the entrance and then into the labyrinth for the first time. As Ofelia walks away from the labyrinth with Mercedes, a crane shot takes us up on top of the entrance archway and stops to view the magical insect. Crane shots of this kind are used within *Pan's Labyrinth* to give the viewer a glimpse of the fantasy to come.

The relationship between Ofelia and her mother is loving and close, and of course it is the last straw for Ofelia's already fracturing psyche when her mother dies. In her mother's sick room, the two are framed tightly together, whether they are talking or Ofelia is soothing her unborn brother with a story. When 'The Book of Crossroads' predicts Carmen's blood loss, the camera tracks forward behind Ofelia and the viewer sees, with her, the terrifying image of her mother covered in blood. Again, Ofelia is presented as our guide via the cinematography and again, what she sees is not safe or re-assuring. After it is implied that the Mandrake baby's presence has tempered Carmen's fever, Ofelia is framed tightly in a close-up where she lays her head on her mother's stomach and begs her unborn brother not to hurt their mother when he is born. Ofelia's head completely blocks any view of her mother, visually predicting a time when Ofelia's family will solely consist of her and her brother. The last time that the viewer sees Ofelia and her mother framed calmly together is after Carmen's fever has subsided. Whether her health has improved because of the mandrake root or her body's natural resistance, Carmen feels better, and is framed symmetrically with Ofelia, playing cards. Unfortunately, of course, in a later scene the hideous close-up of the Mandrake baby writhing and burning is coupled with a close-up on the mother's face in extreme pain. In the last shot we see of Carmen she is framed in the left bottom part of the screen. The camera is tracking around the room and doesn't rest on her, merely allowing the viewer a brief glimpse of her agonised face and blood soaked nightdress. Carmen's progress in the film has been towards a position of absence; from the frame, as well as from her daughter's life.

When Mercedes and Ofelia are framed together, the connotation is of a maternal influence and a place of safety for the child. Mercedes often dominates the frame, but in a caring and protective manner. When she hums the lullaby theme to Ofelia her body seems to surround that of the upset child's. Mercedes herself is often framed alone; taking things out of her secret store hole in the kitchen or signalling the resistance. Unlike when Ofelia is framed in solitary, Mercedes does not appear vulnerable in these shots; she is presented as working within a very dangerous environment, but steadfast and courageous in her pursuit of the truth. After Ofelia's mother has died, she is framed together with Mercedes for the last time (when Ofelia is alive) when they attempt and fail to escape from the Mill. Ofelia is then dragged to the attic by Vidal, hit and abandoned. She is shot in long shot, sitting on her bed and framed by darkness. Devoid of light or comfort, this is one of the most heart-rending scenes in which we see Ofelia. When Mercedes is chased into the forest, she is framed with the Fascists on horseback behind her. She is eventually surrounded and an over-head shot captures Mercedes' trapped position. The frame becomes increasingly imprisoning, with horses behind Mercedes and Serrano in the foreground of the frame. The cinematography here increases tension, only broken when a mid shot shows Serrano being shot by the resistance. The frame around Mercedes gradually empties as the Fascists are shot or ride off; and as her brother enters the frame to embrace Mercedes in mid shot, the viewer realises that she is safe.

As Ofelia enters the labyrinth for her first encounter with the Faun, a crane shot is used to show her progress into this other world. Another crane shot then looks down on her decent into the core of the labyrinth. As she reaches the bottom of the stairs, the crane pulls back and up to leave Ofelia to whatever she is about to encounter. The viewer needs to understand Ofelia's vulnerability and isolation, and the camera movement emphasises this. The viewer's first look at the Faun is through a close-up of it seemingly awakening to Ofelia's voice. It is shot from a low angle and this will remain fairly constant in the film, but the Faun is also lit in a way that adds to its enigmatic and ambiguous status. It is the same colour as the walls around it and its coat of twigs and leaves accentuates the shadows that envelop it. This, the viewer is informed, is not a character whose meaning will be 'revealed' easily, if at all.

As Ofelia first reads 'The Book of Crossroads', light shines down on her from the port-hole-like windows in the bathroom, signalling both the importance of this moment and its fantastical nature. A series of close-ups of the book show the viewer what is revealed, too, and this intimacy is essential in the audience's growing understanding of Ofelia's loneliness and reliance on the imagination. As she enters the base of the fig tree to try and save it from the Toad, Ofelia is shot from below with bright daylight behind her and fairy-like particles in front of her. As she begins to descend the crane shot behind her pulls away to focus on the clothes she has left on a branch. In the Toad's domain the framing is tight around Ofelia to suggest the claustrophobia of crawling around within the roots of a tree. As Ofelia announces to the Toad that she is Princess Moanna and not afraid of him a two-shot is used that places the creature and our heroine in the same shot. The two characters are roughly eye-line matched in this scene (their heads are at the same level in the shot) and this confirms for the viewer that Ofelia is not scared and that she has a good chance of succeeding in her first quest. As Ofelia stoops to take the key from the dead Toad's stomach, this action is shot with a high angle to confirm Ofelia's victory.

49

As Ofelia draws the magic door on her bedroom wall, close-ups of both the chalk and then the magically appearing door outline are used to signal the beginning of the second task, as well as to focus the viewer's attention on the iconography of the fantasy narrative. A crane shot then pulls back from a mid shot, through a dissolve, to a long shot of the diminutive girl about to embark down the corridor towards the Pale Man's lair. The cinematography here clearly emphasises the vulnerability of Ofelia in this task. Mid shots and close-ups of the hourglass confirm that this is a hazardous race against time. The Pale Man is at first seen in a long shot at the head of his table. He is centre shot and yet blocked by the food and the table. This is a monster that will be gradually revealed both to Ofelia and to the viewer. The Pale Man is not seen closely until a tracking shot takes the viewer and Ofelia down the banquet table to him, and Ofelia's shocked expression mirrors the viewer's own. The horror of the scene is evoked further by the 180 degree point-of-view pan that represents Ofelia's view of the grotesque paintings on the Pale Man's walls. Most of the lighting in the scene is generated by the roaring fire. This links the Pale Man to Vidal and also acts to back light the Pale Man, so that even when he is out of focus or to one side of the frame, he is still in threatening evidence.

Ofelia's choice of door is presented in close-up. Both the key entering the locks and Ofelia's face are shot tightly framed. The viewer needs to see that Ofelia uses her instinct to choose the right one, ignoring the advice of the fairy. Ofelia's instinct is one of the significant characteristics that separate her from those characters (i.e. the Fascists) that have devolved responsibility for their actions to an ideology. Once she has liberated the prize from behind the door, the viewer sees the dagger in shining close-up. With the dagger the iconography of Ofelia's quest becomes more frightening and violent. As Ofelia transgresses and takes a piece of the forbidden fruit, a close-up of the fruit and of the child putting the fruit in her mouth, becomes a movement of the camera past her shoulder to focus on the Pale Man. The viewer is then submitted to a horrifying series of close-ups and mid shots in which this monster prepares to attack Ofelia. Oblivious to what she has unleashed, Ofelia is framed in the foreground with an out of focus Pale Man approaching her from behind. (This, of course, alludes to the classic moment of dramatic irony in pantomime – 'He's behind you'.) The Pale Man staggers towards the foreground and into terrifying focus, a focus that then presents him in mid shot and close-up, ripping off the heads of the fairies; as Ofelia runs down the corridor, the camera 'runs' after her and a close-up of the hourglass confirms her perilous situation. As he staggers down the corridor, the Pale Man again becomes blurred at the back of the frame, but as he swipes at Ofelia's legs, mid shots show his monstrousness horribly clearly.

Ofelia tastes the forbidden fruit

Vidal, initially at least, dominates any frame that he is in, whether or not that frame also includes Dr Ferreiro, Carmen, Ofelia or indeed his men. Vidal has many shared scenes with Mercedes, in which he dominates, but only until she has the means to retaliate. In their final conflict, it is Mercedes who overcomes and Vidal is seen from a high angle when she eventually slits his mouth. When his character is being established, Vidal is shot from below and framed against the flames in his room, representative of force. In his room, Vidal is lit to make him stand out from his surroundings and to reign over them. He is framed centrally, in mid shot, grooming himself in front of the mirror. The camera pans around him while he shaves, observing his solitary behaviour. He is framed also against the huge wheel of the Mill in the scene with the rabbit poachers and with an over-turned train at another point, but none of these powerful symbols overshadows him. In the darkness, in front of the Mill, he kills the young poacher and this is shot in a horribly long mid shot, held in order to force the viewer to see his cold barbarity. In the darkness of the barn, Vidal dominates the frames he shares with the stuttering resistance

Vidal from low angle

member. His character is sometimes illuminated by light from the
window, but this is only to show his torture implements more clearly. Vidal
might often be lit, but he is never presented as enlightened.

At the dinner party that Vidal hosts, the camera pans around and down
the table to capture the comments of the guests, of Vidal and the reaction
of Dr Ferreiro and Mercedes to the ampoule of anti-biotic that Vidal
has found. The inhumanity of most of the guests' comments and the
grotesque amounts of food that the panning camera presents, foreshadow
the lair and symbolism of the Pale Man. When the camera does settle, the
symmetrical framing places Vidal at the focal point of the shot, positioned
in front of the fire. Visually he 'pulls focus' and his political comments
have the same impact on his guests. As he begins his diatribe, the frame
empties of other characters and just includes him, the main exponent of
Fascism in the film.

The death of Dr Ferreiro is shot in a particularly startling way. As he
leaves the barn, he is in the foreground of the frame and the camera
tracks back in front of him. Ferreiro is centrally framed and in sharper
focus than Vidal who walks out of the barn after the doctor. In an act of
utter cowardice, Vidal shoots Ferreiro in the back. Still centrally framed
in a mid shot, Ferreiro then stops and falls down out of the frame. He has
helped the stuttering man to die and retained his dignity, but the appalling
manner of Ferreiro's death has revealed yet another monstrous facet of
Vidal.

Camerawork and lighting also establish a sense of place very clearly in the film. The way in which the fantasy environments are shot and lit has been analysed earlier in this section, but it is also important to consider the Mill and the forest as distinct spaces in which events occur. The lighting associated with the Mill is invariably dark, shrouded and sinister. The shapes of the Mill's 'mechanics' throw shadows on walls. Framed in long shots it resembles a place that has been neglected and ill-used; its lack of light being symbolic of its current status as out-post for the Fascists. The Mill was once a place that created life, but now it is the opposite. At the Mill, the darkness is of night-time, but also closed doors and rain. The hiding place of the resistance is not idyllic, but it has more light. The forest is a hiding place, a place of sanctuary and is often depicted with the resistance initially hidden; they then reveal themselves and enter the frame. There are open spaces in the forest that are photographed in long shot, evidencing its status as a site of hope. The caves that the resistance are seen hiding in also act as a contrast to the Mill. Although they have no natural light, the central room is lit by many candles that illuminate for the viewer the many different tasks being done by this unified movement. The light in the cave is shared, unlike Vidal's inferno-like fires in his room that are just for him. The use of light and shadow in *Pan's Labyrinth* has similarities to German Expressionist films. A stylistically radical film movement, most prolific in the 1920s and 1930s, German Expressionist film-makers used sets where perspective was often distorted and extremes of light and shade indicated extreme psychological states. Robert Weine's 1920 Expressionist classic, *The Cabinet of Dr. Caligari*, for example, was ground-breaking in its use of perspective-bending sets to mirror psychological disturbance and F. W. Murnau's proto Vampire film *Nosferatu* (1922) utilised light and shadow skilfully to enhance the menacing nature of the creature. The horror genre is greatly influenced by German Expressionism and *Pan's Labyrinth*'s use of light and shadow, and psychological state writ large in *mise-en-scène*, can also be said to have clear antecedents in this powerful film movement.

In the climactic scene of *Pan's Labyrinth*, Ofelia attempts to take her baby brother to the Faun. In Vidal's room her escape is revealed to him when she moves towards the door and is back lit by an explosion. Although Ofelia has drugged Vidal, the viewer does not see the effects of the drug through his eyes, as this kind of point of view is generally synonymous with the hero/heroine protagonist. It would 'jar' and confuse the viewer at this stage in the narrative to be positioned as the villain. In the labyrinth, both characters are framed either side by the walls and with darkness above. It is only when the walls open for Ofelia, effectively giving her more space in the frame that the viewer is given some hope that she might escape. When talking to the Faun the pattern of high and low angle that has always accompanied these two characters is again evident. The Faun dominates but is no danger to Ofelia, unlike Vidal who not only dominates the frame but also takes Ofelia's brother away, so that she is again alone. A mid shot of the collapsed Ofelia destroys any hope that the viewer may once have had for her survival. As Vidal makes his demand that his son be told about him, he is seen in close-up and this proximity is retained when he is shot in the face; almost to confirm to the viewer that the monster is in fact now dead. As Mercedes sits next to Ofelia, the camera zooms in on the dying child's bloodied hand. A mid shot of the moon reflected in water, with Ofelia's blood dripping into it, is followed by a tilt up the central column of the labyrinth to show that her blood is dripping on this, too. As Mercedes hums the lullaby to Ofelia, the camera pans around her and this is followed by a mid shot of the dying Ofelia. One of the film's narratives is ending with the barbaric death of the child, but also the implied victory of the resistance movement. However, as has already been discussed, *Pan's Labyrinth* is a film in which the resolution of the fantasy narrative attempts to offer solace to the viewer who is horrified that the film has let a child die. In terms of cinematography and lighting, the fantasy resolution is introduced through a golden light that engulfs Ofelia. This light is coded as transcendent, and after this 'golden edit' the viewer sees Ofelia in mid shot, in the fantasy kingdom. A long shot from behind Ofelia presents the triptych of thrones that signal her position in the kingdom. The scene is bathed in golden light and a series of mid shots introduce Ofelia's mother and father as the King and Queen. Ofelia remains at the centre of the court and the frame for this scene. Although she is shot from a high angle, this does not signify submission or vulnerability, but rather the scale of the court and the importance of Ofelia's new role within it. The golden light once again is used as a transition back to the wounded Ofelia, who dies in close-up, and in 'reality'.

Sound

The sound elements of any film are imperative to its success, in terms of generation of messages and values, genre identity and viewer response. To study sound effectively, the student of film must investigate all aspects of both diegetic and non-diegetic sound. What occurs in the dynamic between sound and the other micro elements is of crucial consequence and what occurs between non-diegetic and diegetic sound is of equal importance. Ambient sound, dialogue and aural motifs all contribute to the diegetic sonic palette of a film, as do character themes (these can also be diegetic), soundtracks, voice-overs and sound special effects within the non-diegetic world of the film. Sound elements can also move fluidly from the diegetic to the non-diegetic. A sound-bridge, for example, can be diegetic, non-diegetic or a mixture of both.

The ambient sounds of birds, bees and a trickling stream, for example, create a very different backdrop to a scene, than machinery noise and the scraping of metal. Of course, ambient sounds can be used contrapuntally with action and dialogue if particular meaning is required, so ambient backdrops can not always be 'read' literally. If, for example, the industrial roar of machines and the crackle of sparks that provide a context for the final violent confrontation between Arnold Schwarzenegger's terminator and the T-1000 morphing robot at the end of James Cameron's 1991 film *Terminator 2* were replaced with sounds of waves and ice-cream vans, neither the meaning of the scene or the genre of the film would be clear.

Dialogue functions to present character motive, psychological and emotional reality, and can signal points in a narrative. Darth Vader's revelation to Luke Skywalker that 'I am your father', for example, in the climactic scene of *The Empire Strikes Back* (Irvin Kershner, 1980) not only clarifies a suspected enigma, but also problematises the relationship between hero and villain in the film's narrative. Bryan Singer's 1994 film, *The Usual Suspects*, centralises a story told by the character of 'Verbal' Kint who constructs a series of plausible falsehoods, only revealed as such at the very end of the film and thus uses speech and dialogue to manipulate the audience.

Aural motifs are a powerful way of signalling the presence of a character or the onset of a particular pattern of events. The hiss of the snake, in *Harry Potter and the Chamber of Secrets* (Chris Columbus, 2002) is coded as danger, whether it is on-screen or off-screen. The metallic sound of a coin being tossed signals the presence of Two-Face in the 1995 Joel Schumacher film *Batman Forever*.

In terms of non-diegetic sound, character themes can be used in multiple ways. They can represent sonically the particular characteristics, narrative role and psychological state of a character. A character theme can imply the impact of one character on another if it is heard in a scene where the character that is 'themed' is not present. Character themes often shift between different keys and arrangements within a film to connote the different stages in a character's narrative journey. The lullaby theme within *Pan's Labyrinth*, for example, changes during the film and acts as a kind of barometer for Ofelia's narrative progress.

Analysing non-diegetic soundtracks (which, of course, include character themes) allows the film 'reader' to identify many pieces of information. Soundtracks can help with genre identification, with understanding and immersing in periods of history and with registering the narrative stage of the scene. Our expectations of soundtracks for action films, for example, are that they are fast paced and exciting. Elizabethan court scenes often have a variation on the madrigal as their score. The pace and intensity of the music within a climactic scene will usually be diluted to identify the resolution sequence. Soundtracks are not always musical; they can be cacophonous, discordant and sometimes nothing like our usual expectations of a score. The soundtrack of *Innocence* (Lucile Hadzihalilovic, 2004), for example, offers a sonic backdrop that is akin to a low boom or the drone of a machine. The effect is highly disturbing, because it lacks musicality or variation.

Sound-bridges take either diegetic or non-diegetic sound across an edit to link the meaning or action within a scene. They can be insistent in their attempt to connect characters and events. Contrapuntal sound presents action that seems in conflict with the soundtrack that is heard. Sometimes the intention of a film is to present a clear relationship between sound and action, but the outcome is contrapuntal. D. W. Griffith's 1915 film *Birth of a Nation*, for example, presents images of the Klu Klux Klan riding into town to liberate the white characters from the marauding blacks. The ideological position of the film is that the Klan are heroic liberators and the extract from Wagner's 'Ride of the Valkyries' that accompanies them on the soundtrack attempts to cement their heroic position within the narrative. Of course, having racists as the heroes is ideologically repellent to the vast majority of viewers today, who will read the relationship between the soundtrack and the action as contrapuntal and possibly even ironic.

Voice-overs can set the scene by telling a story, as with *Pan's Labyrinth*. They might identify the character whose journey we are about to follow. Lester Burnham's description of the mundane nature of his world opens *American Beauty* and signals the diegesis as being from his point-of-view (even though he is dead). Voice-overs can present a reliable or unreliable narrator ('Verbal' Kint, again) and thus have to be considered in the same critical way that all other micro elements should be. The post-production sound choices made for a film also include special effects. Is a sound to be amplified, modified or distorted to create meaning? Gun fights, for example, are often enhanced in post-production to create a particular effect. The opening of Steven Spielberg's *Saving Private Ryan* (1998) constructs an environment where the viewer is forced to encounter the tearing force of bullets from above and below the water during the D-Day Normandy landings. The confrontation between Robert De Niro's 'crew' and Al Pacino's police unit outside the bank in the climactic gun battle of *Heat* (Michael Mann, 1995) is an onslaught of violently loud automatic weaponry.

The use of sound within *Pan's Labyrinth* is subtle and complex. The central musical motif was created by composer Javier Navarrete as a lullaby, a form appropriate to the theme of innocence within the film. Lullabies are simple, repetitive and easily remembered. The score is also plaintive and reminds the viewer of both the situation of Ofelia and those resisting the onslaught of Fascism. The score is saturated with sadness and evokes the themes of childhood and loss at the heart of the film's narrative. Structurally, the lullaby score might also represent a feeling of being trapped and isolated and of great sadness. The central refrain repeats and does not resolve. It becomes a beautiful musical prison. There is one point in the film where the lullaby becomes diegetic and that is when Mercedes sings it to Ofelia. After Ofelia is relegated to the musty attic room, supposedly in order to keep her mother calm, she turns to Mercedes for solace. Ofelia asks for a lullaby and Mercedes hums a beautiful, soothing version of the piece in order to try and calm the child. This music soothes Ofelia, as do the caring, maternal presence of Mercedes and the fairy story narrative of the film. The lullaby theme has different tones and is used to create different atmospheres throughout the film, but it is always difficult to escape it or resolve it. The fairy tale motif is clear within the soundtrack, as it is within the diegetic sounds of the fairy story world. The dialogue is rich in the rhetoric of violence, submission and resistance, as well as in the language of love and loss.

Pan's Labyrinth opens with the non-diegetic sound of the signature lullaby. This is coupled with the diegetic sound of Ofelia's dying breaths. Through Ofelia's eyes, we see the fantasy world and, also subjectively, hear the fairy story that motivates the fantasy narrative. Even when the *mise-en-scène* shifts to the real world, the fantasy voice-over continues. This will obviously be a film in which fantasy and reality impact upon each other. The necessity of the fantasy world for Ofelia is immediately evident. Although her mother tells her 'You're too old to be filling your head with such nonsense', Ofelia needs these stories to escape from her fears about her new life with Vidal. The soundscape of mother and daughter in the car also contains a prediction of the mother's fate. She retches and thus straight away introduces the difficult pregnancy that will eventually cause her death. The diegetic sounds of pain reach their extreme with Ofelia's mother when she is later heard screaming whilst giving birth. Her screams stop, and her baby begins to cry, in a combination of diegetic sounds that symbolises the destruction of the state in order to bring in a new order. As Ofelia moves away from the car and towards her first encounter with the fantasy world, the diegetic sounds of the fairy tale are introduced. She sees an insect and the soundscape reduces to the flutter of its wings.

Ofelia's mother's diegetic dialogue is full of the language of submission. She has already capitulated to the control of Vidal and wants Ofelia to do likewise: 'I want you to call him Father… It's just a word, Ofelia, just a word.' Of course, it is not just a word, but a choice to submit to Vidal's world view, one that is introduced by Vidal's first words – 'fifteen minutes late' – cold, detached and controlling. If the opening dialogue presents the submissive mother and the icy Fascist resolve of the step-father, the first words uttered by Mercedes present her as caring, protective and maternal. As she watches Ofelia move towards the labyrinth she warns her 'better not go in there, you might get lost'. Ofelia's response is to explain to Mercedes that the Captain is not her real father. She explicitly denies connection with Vidal, in a statement of choice. This denial of the narrative position and power of Vidal continues right through the narrative and culminates in his denied request at the end of the film. He demands that Mercedes tell his son 'what time his father died' (in an echo of his relationship with his own father), but Mercedes responds with 'He won't even know your name'. To exist in a story is to continue to have power and the resistance denies him that.

Storytelling is an important structural element within *Pan's Labyrinth*, as well as being a way to discuss what should and should not be lauded in history. Although Fascism in Spain continued to be part of the national narrative until 1975 (with the death of Franco), this film's resolution demands that Vidal be denied his place in his son's story. Ofelia not only exists within the two stories of the film, but she tells stories, too. She tells a story to her unborn brother to try to settle him down. She reads fairy stories, tells them, and, as her psychological state becomes more and more fractured, she becomes the heroine within one. When Ofelia is killed, the fantasy story continues and confirms her right to be part of an ongoing story. Innocence, rather than brutality, must persist, the film insists.

Vidal's character has a very specific set of diegetic sounds that continually confirm him in his role of the monster. He ignores the truth of his prisoners' assertion that 'we're just farmers' and crushes the younger farmer's face with a bottle. We hear the crunching of bone and the hard clunk of the bottle in what is a horrible scene of pointless brutality. In his quarters, Vidal listens to big band music, draws deeply on cigarettes, clinks his glass as he pours whiskey and is continually framed in front of a roaring fire. His room is a place not only where the viewer witnesses his enjoyment of the indulgences that he denies to the people of the area, but it is also hellish and inferno-like. At the dinner party that he hosts, the Fascist rhetoric is clear. Vidal states that 'These people hold the mistaken belief that we are all equal. But there's a big difference. The war is over and we won.' His ideology dominates. It is questioned later on in the film by Dr Ferreiro, when he states, 'To obey – just like that – for the sake of obeying, without questioning, that's something that only people like you can do, Captain.' Ferreiro challenges Vidal and at the same time critiques an ideological standpoint that demands submission. Of course, the doctor's challenge leads to his death. Vidal's personality and his politics do have a huge impact on the other characters prior to his death. A sound-bridge is used, for example, between a scene of Vidal in his quarters and the scene where Mercedes says goodbye to Ofelia. Before the sound-bridge, Vidal has stated to Mercedes that 'You must think I'm a monster' and it is as if the idea of the monstrous and monstrous impact is being shown through the use of the sound-bridge. The messages and values generated through the micro elements in *Pan's Labyrinth* are clear – a political system that denies freedom is moribund, but it can be insidious and infecting while it lasts.

The sound within the fairy story narrative functions to absorb the viewer into that world, suspend their disbelief and identify with Ofelia's journey. In terms of actual chronology, the first time Ofelia experiences the magic of the fairy world is when she sees the insect transform into a fairy. This sequence is accompanied by woodwind instruments and ascending notes. The music is expressing the imaginative flight that the viewer has begun to take. Ofelia's feelings on her first entry into the labyrinth are mirrored by the soundtrack. The high notes used at the beginning of the scene evoke excitement and intrigue. The tone then changes when the spiralling note patterns of violins enter to inform the viewer of the potential danger within this place. As Ofelia arrives at the centre of the labyrinth, the lullaby signature is re-introduced. This time it is strong, loud and definite: signalling the beginning of a new stage. Of course, there is danger in the labyrinth, as well as excitement and this is indicated clearly by the sound of a crashing symbol that accompanies Ofelia's descent to the Faun.

The Faun is introduced through the diegetic sound of a growl. It creaks when walking and its associated sound immediately signals it as other-worldly and not human. This is made concrete by its statement, 'I am the mountain, the woods and the earth.' The Faun's initial impact is not terrifying, but it is certainly disconcerting, only tempered by the magical twittering and fluttering of the fairies. The Faun is Ofelia's narrative guide within the fairy story and, as such, its dialogue is full of explanations, prophecies and challenges. Its very first statement to Ofelia of – 'It's you. It's you. You've returned' – presents both the reader and her with a possible alternative story to the one evolving in the Mill. The sounds of the labyrinth itself are primal. Echoes, dripping water and winds all lead us to read this place as primitive.

The sound elements within Ofelia's first quest are almost entirely diegetic. As she moves towards the tree, the squelch of the mud signals the inhospitable and earthy nature of the Toad's lair. The non-diegetic soundtrack comes in as Ofelia enters the base of the tree and underlines the environment as ominous and threatening. The toad is introduced with the same kind of diegetic growl or roar as the Faun had been. Here, the sounds of the monster are amplified for effect: the sound of the slimy tongue, the clicking of its eyes and the revolting eating noises are all exaggerated to promote the fairy tale credentials of the scene. The toad is eventually destroyed, but as a devouring, greedy, life-denying force its symbolism for Fascism is clear.

Ofelia's entry into the lair of the Pale Man is clearly signalled by the diegetic and non-diegetic sound as extremely dangerous. Gothic horror elements pervade the scene and exist also in the sound. As Ofelia enters the corridor leading towards the Pale Man's dining room, diegetic and non-diegetic sounds combine to create an atmosphere of dread. The sonic wallpaper of the scene includes wind and other high-pitched noise, which combines with the diegetic sound of footsteps and sand running through an hourglass, to depict an intense and ominous gothic environment. Once in the Pale Man's lair Ofelia carries out the task, but then transgresses. This transgression is registered sonically in the scene, as well as visually. As the Pale Man awakens, the notes of the stringed instruments on the non-diegetic soundtrack begin to descend in an eerie premonition of the danger to come. The diegetic sounds of the fairy wings and their squeaks build to a frenzy as Ofelia strays from her instructions and eats the fruit from the Pale Man's banquet. The punishment for Ofelia's transgression is visited on the fairies, whose squeaks and flapping become ever more frantic until two of them are decapitated by the Pale Man. Ofelia embodies the wilfulness and impetuousness of youth that is a core component to any fairy story narrative. The diegetic sound of the Pale Man is the most horrifying of all. His brutality and bestiality exceed that of the Toad and this is embedded in his loud, inarticulate and primeval roar.

Ofelia's final meeting with the Faun and therefore the final part of her quest brings together sound themes that the viewer has experienced previously in the film. The diegetic dialogue in this scene sees Ofelia protect her brother from the suggested sacrifice and submit herself instead. When Ofelia denies the Faun her infant brother, its diegetic threatening growl can be heard. Whether the Faun is a force for good or bad, or an ambiguous mix of the two, is still not clear at this point. As for Vidal, his package of associated sounds has come to include that of weaponry and his penultimate scene is no different. He shoots Ofelia and the noise of this brutality is incredibly shocking. As Ofelia collapses, the lullaby theme is re-introduced, this time re-orchestrated to be incredibly tragic.

The sound elements of *Pan's Labyrinth* act as a connective mechanism between the fantasy and the real worlds within the film. The lullaby theme is used in both of the narratives. Similar patterns of diegetic sound are used in the real and fantasy worlds; the inarticulate destructive roar of the monsters in the quest narrative mirror the repeated roar of gun-shot associated with Vidal. Both of the narratives suggest ideological discussions about the nature of freedom, both present the sacrifice of innocence and both propose the redemptive power of that sacrifice. Both Javier Navarette's score and the diegetic sound within the film connect one narrative to another and unify the messages within the film.

Editing

Editing choices are about organisation; organisation that creates meaning. Whether images are placed in a chronological, non-linear or seemingly unconnected order, there will be a reason behind the choice. To analyse editing it is important to address not only how individual scenes and images move from one to another, but also how the different strands of narrative within a film are related, as well as the movement of the film as a whole.

In terms of transition types, an editor has a number of different choices at their disposal. Whether a cut, a fade, a dissolve or a wipe is used will effect what meaning is generated. Cuts are the most common types of edit. Sometimes called the 'Hollywood edit' because of being ubiquitous in mainstream film-making, cuts are the least visible way of moving from one image to another and therefore less likely to break suspension of disbelief in the audience. This rule is, of course, broken when jump-cuts are employed and French New Wave films, such as *à bout de souffle* (Jean-Luc Goddard, 1960), use jump-cuts self-consciously to jar and challenge the viewer. The use of a fade up or fade down tends to signal the beginning or end of a particular section of a narrative. Dissolves, which effectively place two images on the screen at the same time, are often used to signal a connection between two particular elements within a film text. A wipe, which pushes one image sideways, upwards or downwards off the screen, is less common in narrative film. More often seen in music videos, the visibility of a wipe tends to break suspension of disbelief and invite the viewer to register the mechanics of a film or video. Film-makers can use *mise-en-scène* to 'hide' an edit and later on in this section of analysis we will see del Toro's use of pans past trees and walls to mask the cut to another scene. Whatever the transition type, however, it is important to consider the relationship between what is seen either side of an edit and this relationship can be synchronous or juxtaposing.

Continuity and montage editing are the two main structures for organising the different parts of a film. Continuity editing attempts to approximate the linear chronology of actual time; even though ellipsis is used within many films to jump forward through time that is not pertinent to a narrative – e.g. 'Two years later' – time is still moving in a way that is expected. Events still move forward in time and the narrative drive is, therefore, towards the end of the film and conclusion. Within a continuity narrative, flash-backs and flash-forwards can be used, as the dominant movement is still linear. There are, of course, films that break with this forward movement, such as Quentin Tarantino's 1994 film *Pulp Fiction*, but even this includes whole narratives – they are just presented in a non-linear order. Montage editing places many, often disparate seeming, images next to each other in order to create meaning. Montage editing can be used to signify dream sequences or sequences of chaos. The images will have a connection, but this is often thematic or atmospheric, rather than in literal terms of time and narrative. Montage sequences can be used for distribution purposes and often exist in trailers to give snapshots of the action, tone and genre of a film.

Parallel editing is common to feature (and other) films, and takes the viewer back and forth from different storylines in order to construct connections between the two. Parallel edits often jump from different places and events that are happening at the same time to predict an eventual merging of the two narratives. As has already been mentioned, suspension of disbelief is crucial to the audience's immersion within a film and it is not just certain types of transition or editing pattern that can break this. Sustaining eye-line matches across an edit, which confirms that two characters are in the same space having a conversation, is essential if the film-maker wants to retain audience involvement.

The main transition type in *Pan's Labyrinth* is the cut. It allows the audience to suspend disbelief and absorb themselves within the world of the film. Cuts are used in the film to move back and forth between the two narratives in the 'real' and 'fantasy' worlds, to show the impact of events in each and to create the horror and tension within the film. In the lair of the Pale Man, the pattern and speed of the cuts generate almost unbearable tension. The viewer understands that this task is a 'race against time' from the cuts back and forth to the hourglass. The editing in this quest is initially quite slow, allowing both ourselves and Ofelia to take in the scene. The cuts only gradually reveal the Pale Man, which renders him more threatening. Ofelia is shown looking at the table, then a cut to her point of view of the hideous paintings, then a cut to her successful attempt to choose the correct box. The viewer is aware of the danger within the scene, but the editing at this point, depicts her as careful and following instructions. As Ofelia transgresses, however, and eats the fruit, the edits begin to create a real sense of danger. After she takes the first piece of fruit, the cut brings the Pale Man into focus and the viewer is forced to watch his gruesome preparation for attack. A series of shot-reaction shots then show the Pale Man's decapitation of the fairies and Ofelia's terrified face. The cuts accelerate as the Pale Man pursues Ofelia and only calm when she is back safely in her room.

Fades can be effectively used within storytelling to introduce different parts of a narrative. The first fade used in *Pan's Labyrinth* is through the injured Ofelia's eye at the very beginning of the film. The fade is to black as we travel through her eye and up again to the fairy kingdom, clearly signposting the beginning of the first part of the story. The film also uses fades to move between the fantasy and the real worlds. The image of the young girl, running up the spiral stone staircase away from the fantasy kingdom, fades to a ravaged church and then to a human skull. All of these fades are linked to a camera movement, in order to produce a fluid transition from one image to another. Here the camera pans right, as if through a wall, into another scene. This use of the fade is a signature within *Pan's Labyrinth* and can be interpreted in a number of ways.

Because the panning seems to occur in front of the action of one scene, through a wall or a tree and into another scene, it creates the impression that the viewer is standing in front of events, almost as if they unfold on a stage, and gives the film a theatrical feel. It also generates an impression that the viewer is being given glimpses of different, fully formed worlds. In terms of parallel editing, this fading through parts of the set links different areas of action. A series of fades is also used when Ofelia tells her unborn brother the story of the rose. Again a camera movement begins the fade – here it is a tilt down – and again a different arena of the story is introduced. Here we see inside Ofelia's imagination. However, this type of fade is not only associated with Ofelia. Scenes in the forest of the Fascists hunting the Resistance also use this technique and again make clear links between the different narratives.

Pan's Labyrinth is essentially continuity edited. Although the viewer's first encounter with the story is at its end, with a dying Ofelia, the progress of the rest of the film is forwards in chronology; it is an unravelling of the events that lead the child to her death. The story of the Princess and the fairy kingdom acts as an arc for the film. We see the Princess leaving the kingdom at the beginning and at the end she is reunited with her family. These fairy kingdom sections bookend the film, providing a pattern of organisation that gives a positive outcome for Ofelia. They are not used to parallel edit during the course of the film and thus stand alone, the suggestion being that they are not the reality of the piece.

The main body of *Pan's Labyrinth* parallel edits between the world of the Mill, that of the forest and that of fantasy. The scenes at the Mill are edited in an order that presents the increasing horrors that Ofelia faces in her everyday reality. Although her scenes with Mercedes are initially comforting, the organisation of Ofelia's scenes at the Mill gradually empties her world of any comfort. As she becomes more isolated, the number of fantasy sequences increases, indicating her isolation and anguish. It is significant that Ofelia's response to being told that she is too old to read fairy stories, is to immediately begin to imagine one. Her journey towards the Mill at the start so unsettles her that she sees the fairy/insect for the first time. After her thwarted attempt to escape, the Faun appears in a rare scene where he gives Ofelia comfort; and, of course, seconds prior to her death, Ofelia imagines her entrance into her parents' kingdom. The quest scenes are organised into a pattern of escalating danger. As with classic fairy stories, the tasks become more hazardous and each time a task occurs, the parallel editing presents a scene from the real world that has similar meaning. The scene with the Toad, for example, is punctuated by scenes of Vidal hunting the resistance in the forest, followed by his dinner party. Contrasting Ofelia's attempt to overcome a creature that is slowly destroying the roots of the fig tree with the Fascists' efforts to overcome the rural community, demonstrates the different types of resistance acted out by Ofelia and the men in the forest. Placing the Toad's corpulence and greed next to that of Vidal's dinner guests is another clear parallel.

Special Effects

The study of special effects is an important part of textual analysis; especially so when considering films that rely on creating other realities and worlds. The possible uses of special effects are incredibly diverse and not all special effects even today are entirely reliant on computer technologies. Stop motion animation, for example, still has an award-winning exponent in the *Wallace and Gromit* films, which take years to make and are meticulous in their creation of character and place. CGI, or computer generated imagery, is, however, the dominant force behind special effects today; as a means by which whole films can be created (e.g. *Shark Tale* [2004], *Happy Feet* [2006] and *Ratatouille* [2007]) or used to create settings for action that would be either too expensive or hazardous to work in or do not exist (e.g. *The Golden Compass* [2007] and *Harry Potter and the Half-Blood Prince* [2009]). The process of green or blue screening allows the film-maker to project action onto a background that was not there in the first place and is often used in conjunction with CGI techniques.

Not all films create creatures on a computer. With animatronics an animal or part of a creature can be created mechanically and electronically and then controlled remotely. The *Jurassic Park* series (1993–2001) used this technique to create some of their creatures alongside CGI. If the film-maker is attempting to create a human or animal-like creature in a computer, then its reality effect will be partially dependent on the way it moves. Motion capture technologies allow special effects creators to highlight key areas of a human or animal body with sensors that then feed information about movement to a computer. The information about this 'authentic' movement is then stored and used to create a virtual creature or human. Ang Lee's *Hulk* (2003), for example, used motion capture technologies to create not only the Hulk character, but the monstrous dogs that we see in the film. Prosthetics are usually latex additions to the face and body that change the look of an individual or make them seem like another creature. This type of special effect is not just used in fantasy film-making; Nicole Kidman wore a prosthetic nose to play Virginia Woolf in Stephen Daldry's 2002 film *The Hours*.

Special effects can have a dual impact on the viewer. They can help to create a fantasy world that is so beautiful and fascinating that the viewer willingly suspends all disbelief in order to gain access to that world. They can also clearly signal the difference between one world and another in order to present particular messages. These two effects are by no means mutually exclusive. *Pan's Labyrinth* is a film that uses special effects elements in a fascinating, jarring and visually seductive way. These effects do not diminish the messages of the film, but in fact make them more intense and powerful. Special effects are used in this film to create insects, fairies, a baby in the womb, blue flowers, a Faun, a Toad, a Pale Man, the walls of a labyrinth, a fairy kingdom and a small white flower.

Although the fairy insects in *Pan's Labyrinth* are computer generated, they were based on the exact elements and proportions of a real insect. A model of a stick insect was created first and used as a template for the eventual creature. The fairies that the insects turn into are not the stereotypical pretty types. Created using CGI, these fairies have wings that look like tree leaves and bald heads. They are helpful to Ofelia and thus function in the narrative in an expected way. However, their appearance has a more ambiguous, gothic edge. The Mandrake baby was created using a combination of animatronics and CGI, its wriggling and writhing were a combination of remote control and computer enhancement.

A combination of computer generated images, make-up, prosthetics and animatronics creates the most dramatic creatures in *Pan's Labyrinth*. The actor Doug Jones plays both the Pale Man and the Faun, and to do this he spent many hours having both make-up and latex applied all over his body. The Faun's body movement is that of Doug Jones, but the eyes, eye lids and ears are animatronic and remote controlled by an off-screen operator.

What we see on the screen is almost completely created by the costume and the actor. This is apart from the Faun's legs, which bend backwards from the knee and do not approximate human legs. Doug Jones's leg, from the knee to the ankle, had to be removed through green-screening. For the Pale Man's legs to be suitably wizened and skeletal, green screening was again used to 'shave off' some of Doug Jones's inside leg.

The Pale Man in pursuit of Ofelia

The sets and spaces within the film are both 'real' and computer generated. The scenes in and around the Mill were shot on specially constructed sets. One of the only actual places (rather than a specially constructed set) is the ruined church, seen at the beginning of the film. The labyrinth is a set, but when Ofelia runs into it at the end of the film and the 'walls' of the labyrinth open up for her, then computer generated imagery was used. The initial plans for the look of the creatures and the locations for *Pan's Labyrinth* were all sketched out in Guillermo del Toro's notebooks prior to production. Del Toro's notebooks did not begin with *Pan's Labyrinth*, but had been in existence for over twenty years and provide an insight into a director whose imagination is incredibly fertile. From the time he attended Dick Smith's Advanced Make-up course after graduation, through his experiences with his own special effects company, Necopia, to his most recent films, del Toro has sketched his imagination; bringing together the stuff of childhood experiences and nightmares, with his own original vision.

Images from del Toro's sketchbook

CHARACTERISATION

Ofelia's role is that of the central protagonist. She is our heroine of the piece. She does not narrate the story to the viewer via a voice-over, but the opening dissolve through her eyes that leads us into the film, clearly signals her 'ownership' of events. The audience has seen a bleeding Ofelia and the *mise-en-scène* of the opening (the backwards movement of the blood up her nose before the story begins) so it is clear whose story we are following. This means that the story is subjective. It is from the child's point of view and, therefore, possibly unreliable. However, what the viewer quickly learns about Ofelia is that she might fantasise, but she doesn't lie.

As has already been discussed, del Toro picked a female child for the central character within his film for specific reasons. In literature there is a great tradition of stories about the quests of children. Charles Dickens's *Great Expectations*, Mark Twain's *Huckleberry Finn* and the *Harry Potter* series all concern the rites of passage of a young boy. Cinema also includes many films that pitch a child against the hazards of the adult world. *Stand by Me* (Rob Reiner, 1986), *This is England* (Shane Meadows, 2006) and even M. Night Shyamalan's *The Sixth Sense* (1999), centralise a child in order to reflect childhood anxieties and the potential dangers within the adult world. The rites of passage that all of these children embark on is fraught and frightening. Ultimately, they emerge from the journey knowing more about the world and better prepared to enter their own adulthood. Of course, Ofelia is not given the opportunity to enter the next stage of her life and in this way her character differs. The weight of the oppressive ideology that surrounds her and the extremity of her loss, coupled with the film's need to sacrifice her in order to bring about a new equilibrium, set her apart from those cinematic or literary children who have a future.

In fairy tale terms, Ofelia is the Princess and the heroine. In the fantasy world that her fracturing psyche generates, she is a lost member of the royal family who is re-found. Her role in this narrative is as the heroine who sacrifices herself for the greater good and is rewarded accordingly. As the heroine in a fairy story, she battles creatures that represent humankind's primal fears and once she has succeeded in her quest, she is re-established in her rightful place, thus bringing about resolution.

Ofelia the Princess

This trajectory is, of course, subverted and denied in the real narrative of the film. Fairy tales often have a child protagonist, not only so that a child reader can occupy that role in their imagination, but so that an adult reader will experience real fear, too. *Pan's Labyrinth* was granted a 15 certificate in the UK and is definitely not a children's film, but it allows the adult viewer to re-enter their own childhood and fight with Ofelia, to want to protect her, to fully comprehend what she is up against and to 'read' her symbolically, too. Ofelia is the Princess, the vulnerable and lonely child, and the state brutalised by an unwanted regime.

The fantasy characters in *Pan's Labyrinth* have plural roles, too. They are the monsters that lie in the dark recesses of nightmares, political allegories and markers for both narrative and genre. Fantasy cinema for adults and children is full of monsters. These might be derived from mythology, as with the extraordinary models created by Ray Harryhaussen for *Jason and the Argonauts* (Don Chaffey, 1963) and *Clash of the Titans* (Desmond Davis, 1981) or from pre-historic times with the *Jurassic Park* series. Monsters might be alien (the *Star Wars* films (1977–2005)) and often the creation of a monster's 'look' is a product of all of these influences. Monsters generally represent the uncontrollable and uncontrolled. Their value systems are alien to ours, as are their needs and motivations. The viewer cannot predict what they will do. It is interesting to note that the historical development of the monster in horror cinema was one of internalisation. Werewolves and vampires, creatures who are 'out there', evolved into psychopaths and sociopaths in adult horror cinema, suggesting that the most monstrous of all is a psychopathology that is alien to our own. Norman Bates (*Psycho* [1960]), Michael Myers (*Halloween* [1979]), Jason Vorhees (*Friday the 13th Part 2* [1981]), Leatherface (*The Texas Chain Saw Massacre* [1974]), Hannibal Lecter (*Silence of the Lambs* [1991]) and Jigsaw (*Saw* [2004]) may well be far more frightening for more contemporary audiences than Frankenstein's monster or Dracula, because their psychopathic crimes have real equivalents that can be read about in newspapers, seen on TV news or researched on the internet.

In *Pan's Labyrinth*, the creatures are benign, malign and, in the case of the Faun, somewhere in the middle. The fairies try to warn Ofelia, but are ripped to pieces by the Pale Man; the Pale Man is brutality personified; and the Faun is helper, as well as bully. The horror of the Toad and the Pale Man is that they seek to destroy that which is attempting to grow. In the case of the Toad, it is the roots of the fig tree that are being destroyed; for the Pale Man children are his victims. Both characters brutalise what is innocent and destroy futures. Both characters are thus coded as Fascism, a political ideology that suffocates whatever gets in its way. The Faun's function is to lead Ofelia to her quests and explain her role in the fantasy narrative. It functions as the unreliable narrator in the film, as neither Ofelia nor the viewer is entirely sure of its motives. The Faun, and therefore the other fantasy characters as well, appear at points in the narrative where Ofelia most needs to escape her own reality and the increase in the frequency of their presence mirrors Ofelia's increasingly marginalised and threatened state.

The character of the Faun is by far the most complex of the creatures and has the biggest role in the fantasy narrative. This creature's 'look' is straight from Greek and Roman mythology and from the out-set, the Faun describes its connection with nature. This connection is described in almost eternal terms and the agedness of the Faun is confirmed visually. It has leaves and small branches seemingly growing all over itself. The mythological Faun was a spirit of nature and this character's representation includes a comment about what is transient and what will remain. Nature will continue despite changing politics. Human beings die, but characters in myths and stories will last much longer.

The Faun is intimately association with nature

Any discussion of *Pan's Labyrinth*'s monsters must include an analysis of the character of Vidal. Actor Sergi Lopez has said that it is unusual in contemporary cinema to have the opportunity to play a character so entirely dark and unsympathetic and it is the case that Vidal seems to have absolutely no redeeming features. He is the villain and his politics are villainous. The film makes this absolutely clear. The character of Vidal is unambiguous and this makes him an appropriate antagonist to Ofelia's heroine. Vidal's character is a composite of extraordinarily brutal characteristics. His only interest in Carmen is the son she will bear him; he dispatches the rabbit poachers without conscience or emotion; and he at no point registers that Ofelia is a motherless child who should now be under his protection. His ideology is manifest. Whether Vidal's pathology existed before he became a Fascist or was formed by it, the film never explains, but he is oppressive ideology incarnate. But this very lack of complexity means that Vidal functions almost like one of the fantasy characters. He is relentless, unquestioning and vicious – all the characteristics the viewer would expect from a monster. Vidal is the Big Bad Wolf of the fairy story and, as such, his role is to threaten the heroine, but be overcome in the end. In effect, this is what happens, but it is the resistance that eventually shoot Vidal, after he has killed the heroine. Vidal's language is clearly Fascistic, as is his physical treatment of other human beings. It is Dr Ferreiro that identifies the subservience at the root of Vidal's allegiance to Fascism, however, when he states that 'to obey –

just like that – for the sake of obeying' is something that only someone like Vidal could do. Characters who question and challenge in *Pan's Labyrinth* are presented as ultimately stronger than those who capitulate to another individual or to a political system. Carmen capitulates to Vidal and Vidal is subservient to his unquestioned political beliefs, but Dr Ferreiro, Mercedes and Ofelia all challenge and question.

INSTITUTIONS

The budget for *Pan's Labyrinth* was 13,500,000 Euros and it was produced by del Toro's production company, Tequila Gang. The production team behind the film were carefully chosen and included those that del Toro had worked with before or were his film-making peers. Director of Photography Guillermo Navarro had worked on *Hellboy* and fellow Mexican director Alfonso Cuaron (*Y tu mamá también* [2001], *Harry Potter and the Prisoner of Azkaban* [2004], acted as a producer. Composer Javier Navarrete also composed for *The Devil's Backbone*. Del Toro himself was writer, director and producer. Filming took eleven weeks, from June to October 2005. It took place in Madrid and the suburbs outside Madrid.

Casting was absolutely crucial and del Toro made some brave decisions during the casting process. Ivana Baquero, for example, was a little older than del Toro had initially envisaged for Ofelia and did not look exactly as he had planned. Sergi Lopez was known as a comedy actor in Spain before he was cast against 'type' to play the brutal Vidal. Maribel Verdu, who plays Mercedes, was best known for playing sultry and seductive characters, such as the female protagonist of Cuaron's *Y tu mamá también*. As with Sergei Lopez, her casting against type proved very successful. The 'continuity factor' in the casting of *Pan's Labyrinth* was Doug Jones, cast as both the Faun and the Pale Man, who had worked with del Toro on both *Mimic* and *Hellboy*.

The classification journey of the film was smooth. The film was submitted to the BBFC (British Board of Film Classification) by Optimum Releasing and classified on 6 July 2006 with a 15 certificate ('contains strong language and bloody violence'), and no cuts. The film's trailer was given a 12A certificate. For the DVD/video release the film received a 15 certificate and the trailer a 12 classification. *Pan's Labyrinth* premiered at the 2006 Cannes Film Festival on 27 May 2006. It was first shown in the UK at the London FrightFest Film Festival on 25 August 2006. Its first general release was in Spain on 11 October 2006. In the US, *Pan's Labyrinth* was first screened at the New York Film Festival on 15 October 2006. It went on to have a limited release from 29 December and a general release from 19 January 2007. In terms of certification, the MPAA (Motion Picture Association of America) designated an R (restricted) rating, meaning that no-one under the age of 17 could see the film without an accompanying adult.

Trailers

Pan's Labyrinth has a teaser trailer and a main trailer, but both of them contain a lot of detail about the film. The teaser looks more like a full length trailer, with the main trailer being an extended version. The teaser attempts to sell the film to audiences in a variety of ways. The genre identity of the film is presented through the narrative fragments and *mise-en-scène*. The fantastical creatures (the Faun and the fairies) that we see, as well as the setting of the labyrinth and the fairy kingdom identify the film as a fantasy piece. But the images of Vidal in his uniform, the dead doctor, the truck, the horses and the guns imply that there is a dual narrative, one set in wartime and one which we can assume will run parallel with the fantasy story. The gothic elements of the film are apparent in the use of colour, especially in the labyrinth, which is a dark and shadowy canvas. The character most evident in the trailer is Ofelia and the potential viewer can assume that she is the main protagonist who will act as our narrative guide. Vidal is also shown, although never in the same frame as Ofelia and with very different associated *mise-en-scène*. He is implied to be the antagonist of the piece. Ofelia is shown with the Faun and the fairies, entering the fantasy kingdom and in bed with her mother. There is a fire and the warmth and closeness of their relationship are clearly established. From the visual association with the fantasy world, we can assume that this will be a film in which this young girl goes on a very special type of journey. This journey is further understood by the question that comes up on the screen: 'What happens when make-believe believes it's real?' The implication is that this will be a film in which fantasy and reality meet and merge.

The sound elements substantiate what the viewer has already deduced about genre. The central lullaby theme begins the trailer, but as the pace accelerates the music takes on a louder, more urgent, tone. Near the end the soundtrack is a full orchestral piece with chants. The trailer ends with the sounds of wind, bells and the sort of organic creaking that viewers of the whole film will know to be associated with the Faun. It is not just the sound that becomes faster during the trailer. The editing picks up the pace with a montage of key dramatic moments. The Mandrake baby is seen on the fire, Dr Ferreiro is shown face down on the ground with Vidal towering over him, Carmen clasps her pregnant stomach in pain and then, in a seemingly incongruous image, Ofelia enters the fairy kingdom. The violence and pain of all but one of these images contrasts with the beautiful fairy tale images seen at the start of the trailer. Ofelia's entry into the kingdom seems to promise a resolution to the pain that has gone before it. The trailer clearly establishes the main themes of the film: childhood, imagination, loss and oppression. Its USP (Unique Selling Point) is the promise of colliding narratives that contain extraordinary visual elements.

The extended trailer contains most of the same elements as the teaser trailer, but with significant additions. It begins with an advertisement for the US distributor of the film, Picturehouse (A Time Warner Company). This is absent from the teaser and adds an institutional reference to the marketing strategy. The voice-over of this trailer is also an addition and sets the fairy tale and fantasy tone from the outset. 'In a dark time when hope was bleak' it begins, using the language of children's stories, as well as an apt description of the wartime conflict that is seen on the visuals. The first images in this trailer are of fighting, explosions, a grey visual palette and a uniformed Vidal. The diegetic sound of guns and explosions can be heard, further indicating to the potential viewer that on one level this is a film about the events and effects of war and conflict. Ofelia is then introduced, in her first meeting with her nemesis, Vidal. The voice-over tells us that in this time 'there lived a young girl, whose only escape was in a legend'. As the viewer hears the word 'escape', we see Vidal grab Ofelia's hand and a non-diegetic drum sound makes it even clearer this man, and what he represents, will be what the child needs to try and escape *from*. This narrative clue then gives way to an indication of the film's critical status. Text appears informing us that the film was an official selection for the Cannes Film Festival in 2006.

Having been offered a potential conflict (Ofelia and Vidal) within the narrative, information about the violence of the historical situation and an indication of critical acclaim, the trailer then starts to lure in the viewer with sound and visuals from the film's fantasy narrative. The beautiful and haunting lullaby theme is used to introduce a montage of images from the fantasy world. The myth and fairy tale elements and fantasy conventions of this film are clear, as are its exceptional production values. The voice-over speaks of 'signs', 'secrets' and 'a journey that will make you believe', and the potential viewer is being made a promise about their own journey within the film. Any effective trailer sets up promises and enigmas, and this one does so extremely effectively. After the visual and aural promises of fantasy worlds, the trailer then returns to critical plaudits in order to try and sell the film; the same quote that is seen on the US poster from Roger Ebert in *The Chicago Sun Times* – 'Beautiful and exhilarating. A fairy tale for grown-ups' – is followed by 'Unrelentingly imaginative' from Gene Seymore in *New York Newsday*.

The trailer then reminds the viewer of the dual perspective of the film. If the USP of the piece is the intertwining of fantasy and reality, then the prospective viewer needs to know something about both worlds. We had feared that Vidal was a destructive voice and here he is seen in violent situations. He is seen in the barn with his prisoner, showing off the torture implements he is about to use. We do not see Vidal actually inflict violence, but the promise of it is there. The trailer then reminds the viewer of the distribution detail of the film: from Picturehouse and Telecinco. It also proclaims 'From the imagination of Guillermo del Toro' in a statement which implies that a signature characteristic of this director's work is the creation of worlds of incredible imaginative force. As this statement is made, there are images of the Pale Man's lair and, especially, of his laden table. The colours in this scene and the seething brutality of the environment reinforcing the claim about del Toro's imagination. The non-diegetic sound of the trailer becomes more and more rousing at this point. It is orchestral, choral and dramatic, promising the cinema audience a film of emotional power. In this quickening montage pain and violence have increased. Vidal slits across his own throat in a mirror image and we hear the heightened diegetic sound of a knife slash. Ofelia takes comfort from the Faun and a resistance member has his injured leg sawn off. The tone has become far more fraught. The same montage used in the teaser trailer is then repeated – the screaming Mandrake baby, Dr Ferreiro dead in the rain, the mother's pain and the kingdom – but it has been extended to include the Pale Man, the insect/fairy, the (mother's) funeral, an over-turning truck, a flower opening its petals, the Fascists chasing the resistance into the woods and Ofelia in the kingdom looking down at her rich clothes. This montage swings the viewer from the fantasy to the real narrative and back again, repeating the pattern that will structure the film. As the non-diegetic sound reaches its crescendo, the final image is of Ofelia, through a low angle shot, back lit by bright sunshine, walking into a haze of fairy particles and dropping down into an underground world. As with the teaser trailer, the viewer is presented with generic, visual and aural snapshots of what is to come. The trailer ends with the film's title, the 'Y' of 'Labyrinth' becoming a root; the lullaby re-starts and the camera pans across the domes of the fantasy world again. We are being left with a hopeful, rather than violent, image.

Details of key crew are used to sell *Pan's Labyrinth*, as is the status of the director himself: the trailer states that this is a new film 'from Guillermo del Toro. Director of *Hellboy* and *Blade II*'. *Empire* magazine is used to substantiate the film's critical credentials: 'Del Toro's masterpiece... Dark, twisted and beautiful. 5 *****.' The film's website address appears at the end of the trailer, signposting the interested viewer to a more detailed reference point for the film.

Poster

The US and UK theatrical release posters both contain essentially the same elements. The posters are structured as if to funnel the viewer's gaze towards the centre of the poster where we see a child (Ofelia), shot from behind. The pattern of concentric circles used in the design of the poster starts with the entrance to the labyrinth. Used like a theatrical proscenium arch, the stone entrance gate with the head of the Faun as the key-stone at the top of the frame, acts to lure the potential viewer in. Although the arch-way is covered in vines and branches, it is shadowed and green with mould; if it has tempted the child to enter, why not the potential viewer? Ofelia is seen on her own, half way between the arch of the labyrinth and a rotting old tree. Her coat, socks and shoes indicate her age, as well as the non-contemporary setting of the film. This will be a film about a young girl's, often lonely, journey, the poster promises (as does the trailer). It will be set in a fantasy world, but the dark, shadowy parts of the poster's *mise-en-scène* imply that this world will not always be safe.

The text on the US poster begins from the top with a quote from Roger Ebert in the *Chicago Sun Times* that gives critical affirmation to the film and also confirms the fantasy and fairy tale elements that have been identified by the potential viewer in the visual elements of the poster. On the UK poster, the endorsement of *Empire*, the UK's biggest-selling film magazine, is given priority (see page 92). As with the trailer, del Toro's name features prominently. But whereas the UK poster also mentions *Blade 2* and *Hellboy*, none of del Toro's previous films are mentioned on the US poster and it is perhaps assumed that the audience wouldn't need that information to understand what this director's work is like; perhaps even presuming an auteur status for del Toro. Although not visible on the version overleaf, on most versions of the poster the tag line 'Innocence has a power evil cannot imagine' also appears – a statement that confirms the film's genre, its themes and its centralising of the imagination.

Website

The *Pan's Labyrinth* website, which unfortunately no longer appears to be available, was a goldmine of information, branded in exactly the same way as the film, the DVD and the posters. The *mise-en-scène* was consistent and so was the sound. The site provided institutional, as well as textual detail and gave an insight from the director into the film's production. Of course, any 'reading' by the film-maker is but one – and not the sole – means to interpret a film, but del Toro's descriptions of the genesis and process of the film are particularly enlightening. The site included images from del Toro's own pre-production sketchbooks, details of casting and other production choices. Much of this information remains available via a simple internet search.

Pan's Labyrinth was extremely successful critically. At the 2006 Academy Awards, it won Oscars for Cinematography, Art Direction and Make-up. It was the favourite to win in the Best Film Not in the English Language category, but lost out to *The Lives of Others* (2006). The film also won 3 BAFTAs for Costume, Film Not in the English Language and Hair & Make-up. At its 2006 premiere in Cannes *Pan's Labyrinth* received a 22 minute standing ovation, and in many critics' top 10 lists, the film was voted No. 1; both Mark Kermode in the *Observer* and Roger Ebert in the *Chicago Sun Times* considered it the best film of 2006. On websites where the reviews are user generated, the film was also roundly praised: it gained 95% on the 'Tomatometer' on www.rottentomatoes.com. The film was successful at the box office, too, accumulating gross profits, to date, of over $83 million (www.imdb.com).

Summary

Having used *Pan's Labyrinth* in A Level Film Studies classes since 2007, I've had first hand experience of its impact on students. This is a film that does not provoke insipid responses. As a text through which to discuss 'emotional response' it is exceptionally productive. Students have been known to cry (of course, by the time the lights go up in the classroom, there is only the tell tale red face and sniff that betrays the tears!). *Pan's Labyrinth* has made students angry, for a variety of reasons which range from what is presented about the Spanish Civil War and Fascism, to the fact that it seems barbaric to let Ofelia die. The violence has shocked and the intricate construction of the fantasy elements has suspended all disbelief. Whether the focus of study has been textual analysis, genre, narrative, institution or messages and values, *Pan's Labyrinth* has provided an incredibly rich source. For my own part, I teach the film and I write about it, but more than that, I am an enormous fan of the beautiful, complicated and challenging world of Guillermo del Toro's, *Pan's Labyrinth*.

BIBLIOGRAPHY

Books

Gamm, K., *Teaching World Cinema*, London: British Film Institute, 2004

Hayward, S., *Cinema Studies: The Key Concepts*, Abingdon: Routledge, 2006

Nelmes, J. (ed.), *Introduction to Film Studies* (Fourth Edition), Abingdon: Routledge, 2007

Noble, A., *Mexican National Cinema*, Abingdon: Routledge, 2006

Propp, V. (trans. Scott, Laurence), *Morphology of the Folktale*, 1928, Bloomington: Indiana University Press, 1958

Todorov, T. and Weinstein, A., 'Structural Analysis of Narrative Author(s)' in: *NOVEL: A Forum on Fiction*, Vol. 3, No. 1, pp. 70-76, Durham: Duke University Press, 1969

Wood, J., *The Faber Book of Mexican Cinema*, London: Faber and Faber, 2006

Wood, J., *Talking Movies. Contemporary World Filmmakers in Interview*, London: Wallflower Press, 2006

Websites

www.panslabyrinth.com (Official site: interviews with del Toro, sketchbooks, production and distribution information) – no longer accessible

www.imdb.com (Internet Movie database)

www.guardian.co.uk (Good for film reviews)

www.rottentomatoes.com (Film reviews and popular criticism)